ANGLES
ON THE ENGLISH-SPEAKING WORLD

VOLUME 7

The State of the Union: Scotland 1707-2007

Editors: Jørgen Sevaldsen & Jens Rahbek Rasmussen

ANGLES
ON THE ENGLISH-SPEAKING WORLD

VOLUME 7

The State of the Union: Scotland 1707-2007

Editors: Jørgen Sevaldsen
and Jens Rahbek Rasmussen

MUSEUM TUSCULANUM PRESS
UNIVERSITY OF COPENHAGEN
2007

Published for
the Department of English,
University of Copenhagen

*

EDITORIAL BOARD

DORTE ALBRECHTSEN   RUSSELL DUNCAN

LENE ØSTERMARK-JOHANSEN

BOOK REVIEW EDITOR
CHARLES LOCK

*

Angles on the English-Speaking World is published once a year by the Department of English at the University of Copenhagen. Issues are thematic and contain a balance of articles from local and international contributors. *Angles* is intended as a lively forum for a broad range of literary, linguistic, cultural and historical studies from various theoretical standpoints.

*

Articles for consideration and all editorial communication should be sent in three copies to:
Angles on the English-Speaking World
University of Copenhagen, Department of English
Njalsgade 130, DK-2300 Copenhagen S, Denmark

Business communications, including subscriptions and orders for reprints, should be addressed to the publishers:

MUSEUM TUSCULANUM PRESS
Njalsgade 126, DK-2300 Copenhagen S, Denmark
www.mtp.dk

*

Cover design by Henrik Maribo based on a hand-coloured engraving entitled *Monde dans une tête de fou* (ca. 1590): Bibliothèque nationale de France.

Set by Pia Theilgaard Smith

Printed in Denmark by KOPI SERVICE at the Faculty of Humanities,
University of Copenhagen

© 2007 MUSEUM TUSCULANUM PRESS &
ANGLES ON THE ENGLISH-SPEAKING WORLD
New Series, volume 7

ISBN 978-87-635-0702-8
ISSN 0903-1723

CONTENTS

General Editors' Preface 7

Editors' Preface 9

Jens Rahbek Rasmussen
Introductory Thoughts on Scotland,
England, Empire and Europe 11

David McCrone
State, Society amd Nation: The Problem of Scotland 21

Steve Murdoch and J.R. Young
Union and Identity: Scotland in a
Social and Institutional Context 35

Paul Ward
'Union is not Amalgamation. Scotland is a Nation':
Unionism and Scottishness in the Twentieth Century 59

Henrik Halkier
Governing Regional Development in Pre-Devolution Scotland:
Thatcherism and the Scottish Development Agency 77

Robert C. Thomsen
Beyond the Cringe:
Scottish Nationalism since the 1960s 95

Graham D. Caie
The Scots Language then and now 109

Karina Westermann
That Dear Green Place Rewritten:
Alasdair Grey and Scottish Literary Independence 117

Charles Lock
Five Passports and a Broken Stone:
Tercentenary Thoughts in Honour of Edward Lhuyd 129

Notes on Contributors 153

Forthcoming Issues 155

ACKNOWLEDGEMENTS

The editorial board of *Angles* gratefully acknowledges the generous financial support for this and the coming four issues of *Angles* from *E. Lerager Larsens Fond*, Charlottenlund, Denmark. Without its support the publication of this issue would not have been possible. We also want to express our appreciation to the Department of English, Germanic and Romance Studies, University of Copenhagen, for subsidising the funding for this issue.

Dorte Albrechtsen
Russell Duncan
Lene Østermark-Johansen

EDITORS' PREFACE

This special issue of *Angles: The State of the Union: Scotland 1707-2007* marks the three hundredth anniversary of the Union of the two kingdoms of Scotland and England under the name of the Kingdom of Great Britain.

When the volume was first planned the editors were in no doubt that the occasion would be duly marked and noted in Britain, even if it would not give rise to any great celebration. The historic relationship between England and Scotland has fluctuated over the years and has always been a matter of interest to Danes, whether as observers or participants. The recent establishment of a Scottish Parliament has created a new interest, not least outside of the British Isles, in the constitutional framework of the United Kingdom, as the state was named after the accession of Ireland in 1801. Is the parliament at Holyrood a harbinger of complete Scottish independence, or will the extended autonomy that the Scottish people now enjoy create a new and sufficient sense of balance within the union, and even bring about a new sense of purpose?

Scotland and Denmark are neighbouring countries, and the North Sea has for centuries been a major trading route for merchants and a source of wealth (sometimes contested) for fishermen and oil companies. As is made clear in one of the essays in this volume, dynastic connections between the royal houses of Scotland and Denmark have been of historic importance. In 1589 James VI of Scotland married Anne, the sister of Christian IV of Denmark. When James became James I of England in 1603, thus embodying in his person sovereignty over two kingdoms, Anne became Queen of both England and Scotland. And when the Kingdom of Great Britain was created in 1707, Queen Anne's husband was a Dane, Prince George.

Along with other continental Europeans in the Age of Romanticism, Danes became fascinated by the Highlands and the legendary past, especially as shaped and presented in the poems and novels of Sir Walter Scott and in the epics attributed to Ossian. Scott's works enjoyed enormous popularity in Denmark, and (as elsewhere in Europe) inspired many works of art by way of respectful imitation. Bournonville's ballet *Sylfiden* (1836) features as the central male role a kilted Highlander. The composer Niels W. Gade made his first public success with *Echoes of Ossian* (1841). The Scots have had a generally good press in Denmark ever since; contemporary links have been strengthened by the decision in 1947 to place the UK office of the Danish Cultural Institute in Edinburgh rather than in London. From the Scottish point of view, there has long been a sense of cultural affinity as well as historical and linguistic kinship with the Nordic world. In the past century many political commentators, notably in the Scottish National Party, have pointed to the Nordic countries as examples of nations able to flourish independently with relatively small populations, in the cases of Norway, Finland and Denmark, and now the Baltic Republics as well. Scots have also been interested in the model of devolution established within the Kingdom of Denmark for its 'overseas territories' of Greenland and the Faroe Islands.

We are pleased to be able to present a volume on Scotland and its place in the United Kingdom that is, as the topic demands, both multi-disciplinary and trans-national, in its concepts as in its contributors. It has been a pleasure to work with English and Scottish colleagues, who have welcomed the project, have responded with courteous efficiency to our demands and deadlines, and have appreciated this enterprise as another opportunity to strengthen connections with scholars in Danish universities. We are of course also grateful to our contributors from this side of the North Sea, known from here as the Western Ocean (Vesterhavet).

In addition to thanking all our contributors, we must also express our gratitude to Dorte Albrechtsen, Charles Lock, Pia Theilgaard Smith and Sofie Bonnen for much help generously given in the production of this volume.

Jens Rahbek Rasmussen
Jørgen Sevaldsen

INTRODUCTORY THOUGHTS ON SCOTLAND, ENGLAND, EMPIRE AND EUROPE

JENS RAHBEK RASMUSSEN

Abstract

The discrepancy in size between Scotland and England may in many ways have worked out to Scotland's advantage, because more money could be spent north of the border without anyone noticing in the south. The Scots also exploited to the full the career opportunities in both the union and the empire; and later they proved very adept in securing from Brussels the funding denied them by Conservative governments. With empire gone, Europe again beckoned ambitious and enterprising Scots. At the same time, however, there have been attempts to conceal the undoubted Scottish enthusiasm for empire which has become something of an embarrassment to a nation branding itself as small, civic and green.

"In bed with an elephant" is a common way of describing the relationship between Scotland and England, and the discrepancy in size has certainly mattered in that relationship. Whether it mattered "more in the democratic fourth century of the union than it did in earlier times", as William L. Miller has argued, is perhaps a moot point[1]. To Miller, in the past a supposedly "equal partnership" obtained between the two crowns, and later between the two parliaments, while now the union "joins 37 million electors in England to 4 million in Scotland" (plus 2 million in Wales and one in Northern Ireland). But population and resources mattered in earlier times too, and were distributed in much the same way: measured by "population, wealth and apparatus of government", the resources of seventeenth-century England "were only augmented by a tenth with the addition of a British dimension."[2] Miller's conclusion that "the brutal population facts mean that it can only be a union dominated by England" would thus be equally true in the past tense. But if the disparity was not dissimilar before and after the emergence of political democracy, it certainly produced different effects in the two epochs.[3]

Historically England's demographic, economic and political dominance meant that it would be she who intermittently tried to unite or at least subdue the whole or most of Britain or the British Isles. Similar initiatives did emanate from the non-English part of the archipelago, but they failed either to establish the required Celtic unity (as in Edward Bruce's attempted conquest of Ireland in 1318) or to win over a sufficient proportion of the English (as in the two Jacobite rebellions of 1715 and 1745).[4] Scottish or Irish attempts to overturn political relations in the British Isles usually had the more limited aim to win or restore independence from the English hegemony (e.g. Scotland 1314 and Ireland 1798).

The union of 1707 made Scotland part of a British state, but however much Scots may have thought in terms of "equality" between North and South Britain (a nomenclature which never caught on, at least not in England), their country was still very much a junior partner. Scotland's share of the population of Great Britain, which had fluctuated at around 15% during the first century of the union, then began to drop, reaching 12% in 1901.[5] It is now just below 9% and is projected to fall further to slightly above 8% in 2031.[6]

However, Scotland actually benefited from the continued (and widening) asymmetry in demographic numbers and national income. With English population and resources being at least ten times those of Scotland, "per capita over-expenditure in Scotland would produce hardly any detectable under-expenditure in England – even if the English had cared to look for it, which for most of the twentieth century they did not".[7] In most of the first two centuries of the union Scottish interests were catered for by the appointment of what was effectively a viceroy – the most famous of whom was Henry Dundas – whose task it was to keep the natives happy, in particular the professional classes in charge of Scottish civil society, which the Union had left relatively undisturbed. After the shift to mass democracy with the Third Reform Act, the creation of the Scottish Office in 1885 meant administrative devolution for Scotland, facilitating the task of being relatively generous to the Scots in terms of public spending without the English finding out. When devolution came, as William Miller has put it, the disparity in size "not only permitted an asymmetric model, it required one". The various solutions offering symmetry – an English parliament, assemblies in the English regions, or a federal constitution – have always failed and are unlikely to succeed.[8]

With the asymmetry in size went an asymmetry of perception. England may ignore Scotland; there was no way that Scotland could or can ignore its powerful neighbour, with or without the Union. England was, to use a fashionable term, the "significant other" against which Scotland hammered out its own identity. (It is more complex to define England's "other", for there was more than one, and sometimes even more than one at the same time – France, Germany, Russia, America, Ireland.) One important consequence was that it was much easier for the Scots than it was for the English to distinguish between their own nation and Britain.

In many areas Scotland consistently punched above its weight. She sent a disproportionate number of doctors, vets and engineers south to England, which only in the second third of the nineteenth century managed to equal the number of Scottish universities (four, all established before 1600). In the late Victorian era an above average number of Scots were employed as writers and editors of newspapers and periodicals in London (and elsewhere). Last not least Scots were overrepresented in the army and the empire. In 1917 a book, only half-jokingly called *The Oppressed English*, outlined the dominance of Scots in the corridors of power and in the top echelons of the military, and asked whether it was not in fact the English who deserved to have the Home Rule then being debated in relation to Ireland and the empire.[9]

Union and Empire in Decline

The access to markets and jobs in the union and in the empire ensured Scottish backing for both until the post-war decline set in and elections from c. 1960 began to produce consistently different majorities in England and Scotland. It was probably not least the empire that helped create national self-confidence in Scotland.[10] When the Scottish National Party was founded in 1934, it wanted "Scotland as a partner in the British empire with the same status as England"[11]. In other words, its attitude was no more "post-colonial" than that of many Irish nationalists before 1914.[12] Instances of pride in the empire and the effort that Scots had put into it could be found long after its demise: in 1996 there were Scottish protests when the Zimbabwe government removed the word "liberator" from a statue of David Livingstone[13].

The union on the other hand was felt by many Scots to be increasingly outdated and useless. This view was not confined to the SNP, but acquired a much broader basis through the Campaign for a Scottish Assembly. Under Margaret Thatcher and John Major the Conservative vote in Scotland collapsed. In 1955 it had delivered half of the seventy-two Scottish seats; the election in 1997 made Scotland a completely Tory-free zone, though they managed to win one seat in 2001 and another (i.e. a different one) in 2005.[14] In the Thatcher and Major years the Conservatives evolved into a largely English party, and the Secretary of State for Scotland was regarded as a sort of colonial governor whose job it was to keep the Scots not so much happy as quiet.

This eventually led the Scots to look for an alternative in "the other union", the EU, which they had not until then been conspicuously enthusiastic about. At the time of the 1975 referendum on membership of the European

Community the percentage of yes-votes in Scotland was markedly lower than in the UK as a whole (58.4% and 67.2% respectively), and several polls over the next years registered a majority in Scotland for getting out again.[15] Many suspected that the Community was dominated by "capitalists, cartels and Catholics", an attitude reminiscent of that of Attlee's post-war Labour government (shared then by the Scandinavian Social Democratic parties). In a political atmosphere where in 1979 one third of all Scots voted for devolution, EC membership perhaps also smacked too much of exchanging one distant, uncaring master for another.

The Appeal of Europe

But on the European issue the Thatcher years saw a sea change of opinion in Scotland. In the words of the American cultural anthropologist Jonathan Hearn, "Scotland's civic nationalism voice[d] a moral critique of neoliberalism and a communitarian defence of the idea of the welfare state, grounding these in Scottish culture and society."[16] One example of this line of thought is found in a lecture delivered in 1995 by the journalist and politician George Reid. Here Reid sketched a distinctive Scottish tradition consisting of "the commonweal of the Celts, the moral responsibility of the Calvinists, the social concern of the Catholics, the humanity of the Labour movement, and the civic nationalism of today" – implying of course that England had been very different all along, and still was.[17]

From 1988 the SNP adopted the slogan of "independence in Europe" and began weighing up the comparative advantages and drawbacks, in EC terms, of being a small independent country or a marginal region in a great power: was having three votes of your own in the Council of Ministers (as Ireland had) preferable to sharing ten UK votes?[18] Did you get more or less out of the structural and regional funds as a region or as part of a state? Even to those Scots who did not favour independence, Brussels seemed friendlier than Westminster. In the run-up to the introduction of the Single Market in 1992, the Commission under the presidency of Jacques Delors was very attentive to regional issues. It was thus possible for enterprising Scottish authorities, who felt that the Conservatives increasingly deprived them of resources, to seek compensation in Brussels. In 1988, the Strathclyde Regional Council (with 85,000 employees administering two and a quarter million citizens) managed to get nearly £ 400,000, a fifth of its annual budget, from EC funds for a regional development project involving infrastructure, job training and investment in technology and entrepreneurial skills.[19]

Seen from Scotland the English Conservatives were being downright hypocritical. In the United Kingdom, as little power as possible should be devolved from Westminster to the regions; in the European Union as little power as possible should be transferred from the nation-states to Brussels. The Conservative MP who warned against further EU encroachments by saying "as unionists, we know what unions mean", rather gave the game away.[20] On the other hand it might be argued that it was easy for the Scots to be sanctimonious, for how would an independent (or for that matter a devolved) Scotland treat its regions?

In the somewhat uncritical admiration of Ireland (whose "Celtic tiger economy" made Scottish nationalists discard the Scandinavian welfare state as the model to imitate) it went unnoticed that the Irish in this respect behaved much like English Conservatives. The contradictions between what the Irish government "preaches in Brussels and practices at home" were glaring. Ireland defined itself as one big region, an option which suited its centralized structures and weak regional identities, and at least initially was very profitable in terms of EU subsidies; but it meant being "all in favour of regionalism at the Community level [but] opposed to any extension of regional autonomy within Ireland".[21]

Scotland will almost certainly face similar problems. To the Orkney Islands, Edinburgh may not seem that much closer or more attentive than London, and if (with or without the Union) they end up as a poor periphery in a booming Lowlands economy, what will the political consequences be now that there are no English to blame? It is true that England and Scotland today are experiencing that convergence which Walter Scott mistakenly thought (and regretted) was taking place in his lifetime, but that convergence may not include regions like the Orkneys – or for that matter Cornwall.[22]

Historical Perspectives

What attracts Scottish intellectuals to the EU is not only its emphasis on "a Europe of the regions" or a greater attention to welfare and justice than neo-Thatcherite New Labour is seen to offer, but also the argument that "with Empire gone, it is now Europe that again presents a theatre of opportunity for ambitious and enterprising Scots".[23]

The operative word here is "again" – just as the devolved Scottish parliament in Edinburgh in 1999 was declared not "opened" but "reconvened". In both cases the message is that Scotland, without (necessarily) repudiating the union, is now once again free of certain constraints forced upon them in 1707. The implied argument in relation to the Continent is that the English are, and always have been, Eurosceptic in a way that is not true of Scotland. There is obviously a good deal of truth in this, but at the same time the argument is clearly overdrawn for contemporary polemical purposes.

The problem is partly historiographical in nature. Over the last thirty years a "New British History" has been created, beginning with the pioneering work of (the New Zealander) J.G.A. Pocock[24]. It has not entirely eradicated the often distorting national perspectives, and problems of nomenclature as well as of substance remain. "England" is still often confused with "Britain", and in Ireland there is reluctance to accept the word "British" even in the supposedly neutral geographical sense ("the British Isles").[25] Nevertheless this as been an exceptionally fertile paradigm and represents genuine progress.

It has proved more difficult, however, to break down the walls erected between British and European historiography, though here too there are signs of change.[26] This insularity has had at least two important consequences..

The first is that the focus on the Anglo-Scottish union for long has made historians overlook that such unions, often called "conglomerate states" or "composite monarchies", were quite common both in 1603 and 1707, though they could take different forms.[27] Most of them are admittedly no longer with us, but that is exactly the point: what is interesting about the British union is not that it is now being challenged, but that it has lasted so long (and may of course last a while longer). By the same token, there is nothing odd or unprecedented in calls for its dissolution, which will probably be "more velvet than even the 'velvet divorce' between the Czech and Slovak Republics – though perhaps even less necessary and even more regretted."[28]

Second, the contrast between the Scottish and the English attitude to Europe has been overdrawn. Nobody is disputing that Scots were traditionally open towards Europe. Before 1707 you would find Scottish merchants and mercenaries everywhere; of the soldiers in Gustavus Adolphus' armies in the Thirty Years War, one in six was a Scot. The "Auld Alliance" (1295) meant, as already touched upon, that Scotland's "other" was not France, but England. And even as Protestantism and the Union brought Scotland into the anti-Catholic and anti-French camp, the Scots were open to influence from the Continent, as evidenced both by the Scottish Enlightenment and the Jacobite connection.

It is equally true that England tended to see the Continent as hostile territory, full of huge populous Catholic states waiting to gobble up plucky little England, probably by means of a Scottish or Irish fifth column.[29] To prevent that it was necessary not only to have a strong navy, but also to create alliances and to be able to buy the necessary military manpower. As late as 1962 Harold Macmillan toyed with the idea of countering the French snub to the British EU application by forming alliances, eighteenth-century style, with other European powers.

But even if Scotland's europhilia and England's euroscepticism both have historical precedents, they can be and are being exaggerated for present-day purposes. England has, on its own or as part of the Union, had long periods of close involvement with Europe; as Jeremy Black has pointed out, the years where England was part of a European empire (of a Roman, Danish or Norman variety) or Britain was associated with Hanover easily add up to more than half of the time between the Roman conquest and the accession of Queen Victoria.[30] Most surveys however tend to ignore the at times intense English involvement in European politics. The Hanoverian connection is seen as a curiosity best left to German scholars to explore, and the continuity with earlier alliances, such as that between England and the dynasty of the Welfen (Guelphs), is seldom noticed.[31].

Conversely, it is difficult to avoid the impression that in Scotland the "European card" is sometimes being played to conceal that enthusiasm for empire which has become an embarrassment as Scotland increasingly is branding itself as a small, civic, green and largely social democratic nation. For if seen from Britain the empire was an instrument of civilization, Europeans (not to mention the rest of the world) often saw it differently. Many of course admired Britain as a beacon of liberty, especially those living under autocratic regimes. But to others the image was that of a brutal and cynical superpower that you could not trust and that used its gold to conquer and bribe its way to world dominion, and there is little evidence that as imperialists the Scots were judged less harshly than the English – if for no other reason than the inability of foreign observers to tell them apart.

Thus Scotland cannot escape the historical legacy of having shared in that British empire which was *"Albion perfide"* to the French, *"Raubstaat England"* to the Germans, and *"den forbandede tyv"* ("that cursed thief") to the Danes whose navy the British seized in 1807.[32] This last event was preceded by a bombardment of Copenhagen which caused international outrage. But even as we commemorate this event, the high moral ground that the Danes used to claim is turning slippery, for it is belatedly dawning upon us that for centuries we too had an empire, complete (in its final phase) with slave plantations in the Caribbean. Not an easy thing to admit for a country that likes to brand itself as a small, civic, green and largely social democratic nation, and one that used regularly to be invoked as a model for an independent Scotland.[33]

Notes

1. William Miller, "Introduction: From Last Empress to First Minister", in: id. (ed.), *Anglo-Scottish Relations from 1900 to Devolution and Beyond* = *Proceedings of the British Academy* 128 (2005), pp. 1-13. – Cf. T.C. Smout (ed.), *Anglo-Scottish Relations from 1603 to 1900* = *Proceedings of the British Academy* 127 (2005).
2. Allan I. Macinnes, *The British Revolution, 1629-1660* (London: Palgrave 2005), p. 1.
3. The two direct quotes are from Miller, "Introduction", p. 2.
4. Michael Fry, *The Scottish Empire* (Edinburgh: Polygon 2001), pp. 7-8.
5. Christopher Bryant, *The Nations of Britain* (Oxford U.P. 2006), table 2.1, p. 49.
6. Whereas population figures in England are projected to increase by 12.5%, in Wales by 10%, and in Northern Ireland by 8%, the Scottish population is expected to decrease, albeit slightly, in absolute numbers over the next twenty-five years (as it has done since 1932 except for a short upward blip in the 1990's). Figures taken from the National Statistics website (accessed 12.03.07)
7. William L. Miller, "Introduction", p. 3.
8. William Miller, "Introduction", p. 3; cf. Bryant, *The Nations of Britain*, ch. 8.
9. Quoted by Linda Colley, "Britishness and otherness: an argument", *Journal of British Studies* 31 (1992); cf. John Kendle, *Federal Britain* (London: Routledge 1997).
10. Michael Fry, *The Scottish Empire*; T.A. Devine, *The Scottish Empire 1600-1815* (London: Allen Lane 2003).
11. T.A. Devine, *The Scottish Nation 1700-2000* (London: Allen Lane 2000), p. 388.
12. Stephen Howe, *Ireland and Empire* (Oxford U.P. 2000), pp. 43-44.
13. *The Scotsman*, 30.8.1996.
14. Ironically the Conservatives got around 20% of the popular vote in the first elections to the Scottish parliament, because these elections were based on proportional representation – a principle which, like devolution, the Tories had fought tooth and claw.
15. M. Keating & N. Waters, "Scotland in the European Community", in B. Jones & M. Keating (ed.), *Regions in the European Community* (Oxford, Clarendon Press 1985).
16. Jonathan Hearn, *Claiming Scotland: National Identity and Liberal Culture* (Edinburgh: Polygon 2000). The quote is from the back cover of the paperback edition, but fairly represents Hearn's argument.
17. George Reid, "Oh, to be in Britain?", The Donaldson Lecture 1995 (http://www.snp.org.uk:80/library/art02.html [accessed 30.08.1996].
18. After the extension in 2005 these figures would be seven and twenty-nine respectively. Scottish independence would of course also affect their influence in e.g. the UN and the G7.
19. P. Jones, "Local government", in: M. Linklater (ed.), *Anatomy of Scotland* (Edinburgh: Chambers 1992), pp. 263-65.
20. Bill Walker, quoted in William Wallace, "National identity and foreign policy", *International Affairs* 67 (1991), p. 76. The official name of the party is of course still "The Conservative and Unionist Party".

21 M. Holmes & N. Reese, "Regions within a region: the paradox of the Republic of Ireland", in: B. Jones & M. Keating (ed.), *The European Union and the Regions* (Oxford: Clarendon Press 1995), p. 231.
22 Allan Massie, *The Thistle and the Rose*, p. 144, 148; Miller, "Introduction", pp. 5-6.
23 C. Bryant, *The Nations of Britain*, pp. 107-108. Bryant sees this Europhilia as largely confined to the intelligentsia and quotes Murray Pittock: "Europe is, like Gaelic bilingual signposting, a chic designer accessory to contemporary Scottish cultural nationalism not altogether sustained in society at large". Murray Pittock, *Scottish Nationality* (London: Palgrave 2001), p. 8.
24 Examples, some of them covering the United Kingdom, some only Great Britain, all of them providing excellent bibliographies for further reading, include: J.G.A. Pocock, *The Discovery of Islands: Essays in British History* (Cambridge U.P. 2006); K. Stringer and A. Grant (ed.), *Uniting the Kingdom? The Making of British History* (London: Routledge 1995); L. Colley, *Britons: The Forging of a National Identity 1707-1837* (Yale U.P. 1992), K. Robbins, *Great Britain: Identities, Institutions and the Idea of Britishness* (London: Longman 1998).
25 This has led to considerable creativity in devising non-offending book titles, e.g. H. Kearney, *The Four Nations* (Cambridge U.P. 1989, 2nd ed. 2006); Norman Davies, *The Isles* (London: Macmillan 1999); Richard S. Tompson, *The Atlantic Archipelago* (New York: Edwin Mellen 1986); J. Kramer, *Britain and Ireland* (London: Routledge 2006).
26 Keith Robbins, *Britain and Europe 1789-2005* (London: Hodder Arnold 2005) is part of a new series, "Britain and Europe". There are to be four more volumes, of which so far two have been published, taking the story to 1300. See also Jeremy Black, *Convergence and Divergence: Britain and the Continent* (London: Macmillan 1994).
27 J.H. Elliott, "A Europe of composite monarchies", *Past and Present*, no. 137 (Nov. 1992), pp. 48-71; Jens Rahbek Rasmussen, "The Danish monarchy as a composite state 1770-1830", in: Nils Arne Sørensen (ed.), *European Identities: Cultural Diversity and Integration in Europe since 1700* (Odense U.P. 1995), pp. 23-36.
28 William Miller, "Introduction", p. 8.
29 Linda Colley, "Small is vulnerable – small is aggressive", in: *Captives: Britain, Empire and the World 1600-1850* (London: Jonathan Cape 2002), pp. 4-12.
30 Jeremy Black, *Convergence or Divergence?*, p. 5. Black here commits the classical English blunder of ignoring the Scottish part of the "pre-history" of Britain: the Hundred Years War counts as evidence of Continental commitment for England, whereas the Auld Alliance does not do so for Scotland.
31 But see now the two first volumes in "Britain and Europe".
32 Thomas Munch-Petersen, *Defying Napoleon: How the British bombarded Copenhagen and seized the Danish Navy* (London: Sutton 2007) will be the first full-scale treatment in English of this event. A brief presentation of his thesis can be found on the website www.copenhagen1807.com. That text will appear in Danish in Rasmus Glenthøj & Jens Rahbek Rasmussen (ed.), *"Det venskabelige bombardement": København*

1807 som historisk begivenhed og national myte ["The friendly bombardment": Copenhagen 1807 as historical event and national myth] (Copenhagen: MTP Press 2007). Besides a number of articles written by Danish scholars, the book carries a contribution by Professor Andrew Lambert (King's College) and a preface by the British ambassador to Denmark, H.E. David Frost.

33 Several of the topics touched upon in this introduction will be dealt with more comprehensively in the essays below.

STATE, SOCIETY AND NATION: THE PROBLEM OF SCOTLAND

David McCrone

Abstract

This chapter explores the character of Scotland as state, nation and society. It reviews the conventional cultural markers making for national distinctiveness such as language, religion and social values, and concludes that there is not a set of 'objective' differences between Scotland and England, its most salient 'Other'. Rather, there is a developing 'Scottish frame of reference' through which structures and processes are refracted so as to make Scotland even more distinct. The creation of a Scottish parliament at the end of the 20th century provides another powerful mechanism through which Scotland and England are likely to diverge.

Does Scotland exist? That may seem like the sort of daft question an academic would ask, or, at best, form the basis for a seminar or conference or even an exam question. There is, however, a more serious question lying behind the seemingly facile one. Let me ask it in another way. Does Denmark exist? It does, after all, have a similar population size to Scotland, around five million, and plainly it is a place on a map. That may seem an equally daft question, and even slightly rude. Of course, you might say, Denmark exists because it is a country – very well then, a state, if you prefer the term. You have put your finger on the nub of the answer about Scotland, which, of course, is not a state in the way that Denmark is. Scotland belongs to the set of countries, territories if you prefer, we call 'stateless' or perhaps preferably, 'under-stated' nations: Flanders, Catalunya, Wales, Euskadi, and so on.

Questions of Identity

What these have in common, and share with many, but not all, states, is that they are 'imagined communities' in Benedict Anderson's term,[1] territories in which most people have a sense of belonging to a common set of experiences, roots, a shared sense of belonging which in some way frames people's social, political and cultural practices; in Pierre Bourdieu's felicitous term, *habitus*.[2] It is a highly personal, and usually implicit, sense of sharing something fundamental with others deemed to inhabit the same cultural space. You might argue: why should we assume such a thing, and is it not somewhat dangerous in that some people will belong and others will not? That is a fair question, but issues of social inclusion and exclusion do not gainsay the possibility that a 'community' exists, a thing of the imagination; to be imagined to be sure, but not imaginary. Even in small countries like Denmark and Scotland we cannot meet and know the other five million souls, but we do have a sense that we and they have something basic in common. That's as may be, the Dane might say, but we Danes govern ourselves, we have government, law, education, a history, a shared set of values,[3] and furthermore, we have been in this part of Europe for a long time. Apply those criteria to the Scots: we too have inhabited our place for a long time (about a millennium), we have a parliament, albeit a devolved one, a legal system, an education system, our history goes back a long way – those 1000 years again – and we like to think we share similar values, of treating people fairly and equally, of being tolerant (these days), open and welcoming.

Behind these assertions lies a big question: than what or, rather, than whom? That is the nub. Who are we comparing ourselves with in terms of these values and identities? In other words, who are we *not*? No doubt Danes will say that they are not Swedes, Norwegians, even Germans, but would protest that we are missing the point in not taking seriously our own sense of self. What we have here is what anthropologists call 'othering', saying who we are with reference to who we are not; which is not to say that we are only defined in these terms. We Scots are, to put it plainly, not English. We have shared these small islands off north-west Europe for about 1000 years with a larger, richer and more powerful, and at times predatory neighbour. And we're not the only ones: so have the Irish and the Welsh. There is an old joke. When God created Scotland, the angels were envious. Here was a territory with a temperate climate, coal, oil, fish. What more could the Scots want? Ah, said God, just wait until they see who they get as neighbours. That old contumacious aspect was nicely caught in a recent political cartoon in Scotland in *The Herald* newspaper, following an opinion poll showing that half of Scots wanted independence, but that more than half of the English wanted Scotland to be independent.

Table 1: Poll Update
(Source: Steven Cramley, *The Herald* November, 27 2006)

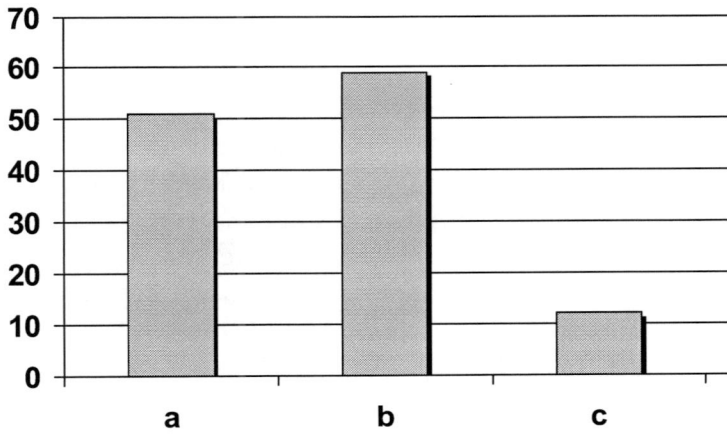

a: Scots in favour of independence
b: English in favour of Scottish independence
c: Scots in favour of independence after hearing English in favour of Scottish independence

Contumacy surfaces again at sporting occasions when we are asked who we are supporting when England is playing: ABE – anyone but England. Is this fair? Of course not. It is largely tongue-in-cheek, but it does contain a key truth. Defining who one is inevitably requires to say who one is not. This does not imply symmetry, of course. The English do not measure themselves against the Scots (or the Irish or the Welsh). The pike does not measure itself against the minnows, which is why the English pay much more attention to the French and the Germans when it comes to 'the other'.

The discussion so far might seem rather trivial and unacademic. It has however a serious point. National identity matters;[4] frequently it is taken-for-granted and essentialised, but when it comes down to it national identity – or better put, the process of identification – is about relating to someone else, positively or indeed negatively. You might object that few of us actually spend time actively thinking about our national identity, and indeed that is true, but that is not to say that it is a trivial matter, confined, for example, to international sporting occasions. In truth, it is a prism through which much of social, political and cultural life is refracted. The prism metaphor is one to which we will return shortly. First, there is another argument we have to tackle, that being Scottish is not actually maintained by anything sufficiently distinctive in terms of the usual markers of national identity.

What is it that makes people Scottish? None of the 'usual suspects' seem to apply, at least strongly enough. Take language. Scots speak English, after a fashion. True, there is Gaelic, the historic language of Scotland until the middle ages, but it was driven back to its north-west frontiers such that today it is actively spoken only by around 2% of the population. It does have iconic status in that the new parliament has bilingual signs in recognition of its historic identity, but, alas, it remains historic. There is a language called Scots, sometimes called Lallans (Hugh MacDiarmid's literary invention) or Doric, a relative of (northern) English, with strong residues in North-East Scotland, and many Scots use Scots words (like bairn, outwith, lug) which derive from Old Norse/Anglo-Saxon roots. Suffice it to say, however, that most of us speak a version of English called standard Scots-English. In any case, English is a global language, and no-one thinks Americans or Australians are 'English' because they speak English. Nor do Scots. Another cultural marker of national distinctiveness has been religion (has been – past tense; Scotland, like England, is in the main a secular society; whereas 51% of people in Scotland claim some Christian religious affiliation, only one in five attends church at least once a month).[5] The Reformation in the 16th century did take a Presbyterian turn in Scotland, in contrast with England where it adopted latitudinarian forms to suit the marital predilections of the monarch Henry VIII: after all, *cuius regio, eius religio*: you got the religion of the monarch, like it or not. When it changed, so did you. Scots from the 16th century belonged to the disputatious family of Protestants, but these days it no longer matters, because few people practise regularly. A thought experiment: if Scotland had, say, been Catholic as in Ireland, religion might well have become a proving ground for political and cultural identity; but it wasn't, and it didn't. Maybe in that regard geography helped – Ireland is an island, after all – but in truth it didn't matter. Sharing the bigger island with England (and Wales) was simply a fact of geography, and the frontier between Scotland and England has been fixed for over 500 years, longer than the one which generated the famous Schleswig-Holstein Question. To complete the indices of national identity: Scots are not obviously visibly different from the English in ethnic terms, though DNA tests suggest that we have a higher percentage of fair-skinned Celts among us, leading, ironically in a country famed for its inclement weather, to higher rates of skin cancer. Cultural practices, apart from those obviously and visibly engaged in to show that Scots are Different, such as kilts, bagpipes, tartan, haggis (many of these of Scandinavian origin), to say nothing of our not very successful sporting teams, do not mark us out seriously enough from the English to make it obvious and self-evident that we are not them.

And yet. We are not Them. If anything, we have become even less like them in terms of identification than ever before. The percentage of people saying they are British has fallen by half to 15% over 30 years.[6] Well over three-quarters of people living in Scotland say they are Scottish. Does it really matter to them? Yes it does. When asked to rank being Scottish vis-à-vis other social identities (class, age, gender, religion – 23 in all), only being a parent comes anywhere near being Scottish; around half. People in England do not reciprocate (only 21% give English), suggesting that being Scottish matters more to us that being English does to them. And it's not a matter of being British. Whereas 27% of people in England give 'being British' as one of their top three choices, only 13% of Scots do so. We have also seen a shift in the relationship between national identity and social class identity. It used to be a common refrain among Scottish Labour politicians that the Scottish working class had more in common with their English counterparts than they had with bourgeois Scots. Social class outranked nationality. We don't hear much of that these days, because over 30 years class identity has actually given way to national identity. Whereas 27% of Scots identify with an English person of the same social class as themselves, 45% identify with a Scottish person of a different social class.

What of people who weren't born in Scotland, or, for that matter, are of a different ethnicity? Around 400,000 people living in Scotland were born in England (around 9%), and Scotland's ethnic minorities number around 2%, mainly of Pakistani Muslim origin. In a recent wide-ranging study, Hussain and Miller[7] argue that ethnic Pakistanis are able to identify as Scots because being Muslim for them is a 'cultural' form of identity, and the most important. Hence, they see no contradiction between being (territorially) Scottish, and (culturally) Muslim. That is why 44% of ethnic Pakistanis describe themselves as 'Scottish Muslims', compared with 23% as 'British Muslims', 15% 'British Pakistanis', and 12% 'Scottish Pakistanis'. Hussain and Miller comment:

> Scottish Pakistanis value diversity. They want a Scotland that is different from its past but different from their past also. They reject a ghetto mentality in favour of a multicultural society in which they would be a respected minority but a minority nonetheless – not assimilated, but integrated. There is little or no enthusiasm for the relatively monocultural society of Pakistan or even that of some areas of England where minorities form a large majority (p. 144).

If Muslims are unwilling to adopt (Scottish) culture, the English seem unwilling to join the territorial nation, given that they were born in England

and are hence 'English'. That is why far more ethnic Pakistanis place themselves at the 'Scottish' end of national identification (49% say they are exclusively Scottish, or more Scottish than British, compared with 10% at the 'British' end of the spectrum). This contrasts with the figures for 'English' immigrants where 62% are at the 'British' end, and only 9% at the 'Scottish'. For people of Pakistani origin, cultural/religious identity is paramount, but territorial identity (being Scottish) can be changed. 'They adopt a Scottish identity easily and quickly. And (territorial) identity, therefore, becomes a bridge rather than a wall' (p.198). The opposite is true for English immigrants. Most feel they cannot become Scottish, but can adapt to what they see as the cultural/religious aspects of Scottish life.

In many ways, we are almost all nationalists now, in some shape or form. That doesn't mean necessarily capital-N nationalists, voting for the Scottish National Party, but it is testimony to a widespread and basic sense of Scottishness across all classes, political parties, genders and ages. It is simply the default position. It was not always thus. What has made this so?

Scotland the Union
There is a prior question we must address. What of the Union, that constitutional arrangement entered into by Scotland and England three hundred years ago this year? The great virtue of hindsight is that we know now what we, or at least our forebears, did not know then. The Union of 1707 was not a conquest, nor a love-match between Scotland and England, but, as the French have it a *'mariage de raison'*, a marriage of convenience between two countries unequal in size and power and riches, but entered into for strategic reasons. For Scotland, it meant access to English wealth, empire and capital; for England, it closed the door to the 'auld alliance' between France and Scotland who would unite in common cause against their enemy, on the Machiavellian principle: the enemy of my enemy is my friend. Scotland retained its institutional autonomy, notably its tripartite system of law, education and religion, its holy trinity, so to speak. It meant that people in Scotland were educated, judged, and worshipped God in a thoroughly Scottish way, without giving much thought to it, just as the Danes, one presumes, did the same things in an unselfconsciously but distinctively Danish way.

For much of the period which followed, Scots carried on much as they had before, being self-governing in matters of the everyday, leaving matters of state, notably imperial ones, to the Westminster parliament. There was, however, an incubus of contradiction lying at the heart of governance. Scotland may be largely self-governing, but as formal democracy happened, so England, with the bigger population, had more clout. The Scottish anomaly – a self-governing territory within a unitary state with a single legislature – became more obvious. Periodically, the Scots would complain about English insensitivities over matters close to Scottish hearts, God and mammon, religion and money, but it took until the middle of the 20th century before the contradictions began to show in political terms. In the first half of the century, Scotland and England voted for the same political parties, Labour and Conservative, in roughly the same proportions. What this did not mean was that both countries were using the political process in the same way. Scotland manipulated the electoral system to look after Scottish interests even if it took the form of ostensibly voting the same way as England. In truth, warfare and welfare were the twin anvils on which people in the 20th century became and remained British. For much of the first half of the century Britain was at war, either virtually or actually. Dying for one's country – *pro patria mori* – was a real possibility for many Britons. The pay-off came in 1945 with the creation of the welfare state, in many ways the price the state had to pay for the blood sacrifice of the previous 30 years. Scots died in disproportionate numbers, probably not unwillingly, but that is an inference too far. They were not unwilling cannon-fodder, and the loss of most of Ireland in 1921 merely served to underline the differences between the two countries rather than their similarities. Many writers have tried to apply the colonial metaphor to Scotland, but it is an ill-fitting suit of clothes. Scots were much more likely to be oppressors rather than oppressed in managing matters of empire.

Social and political change came much later, although the incubus lay at the heart of the Union long before. Scots went along with empire and union because it suited their purposes; it gave them access to power, prestige and wealth out of proportion to what they might have achieved on their own, although one can never tell, given the vagaries of history. In the 1950s and 1960s Scots did not cease to be Scottish, as well as being British; it was not a zero-sum game. Indeed, one could say that these were twin nationalities, complementary rather than competing.

Transforming Scotland

What made it different? In the post-war period, Scotland had to undergo a major process of industrial restructuring away from the staple industries of coal, steel, shipbuilding and heavy engineering which had played such an important part in its economic success over the previous century.[8] The agent for this change was the state, and in the Scottish case, the apparatus of Scottish governance known as the Scottish Office, the institution which had inherited the Scottish boards of education, home affairs and local government, and brought together government departments in the 1880s. After 1945, the 'Scottish state', at least the meso-state, the middle level, was a powerful intermediary between London government and Scottish civil society, and well-placed to manage the necessary economic transformation. This effected major social and economic change, such as an influx of new industries notably in micro-electronics, as well as in public bureaucracy employment. Imperceptibly, the focus, the frame of economic reference, had shifted from London to Edinburgh such that the 'state', including many aspects of the welfare state, took on a Scottish frame. In other words, the 'national interest' was reinterpreted as the *Scottish* national interest. To be sure, this was a shift in degree rather than in kind, as the Scottish boards of education, social welfare and home affairs were augmented by others dealing with economic development and planning. By the late 1960s when public appetite for state intervention and proactive planning was at its height, Scottish civil and political society was readily receptive to political transformation, and it came in the related bandwagons of North Sea Oil and the Scottish National Party.

If Scotland had stayed in the Union, and indeed prospered, for economic advantage within the Empire, then its demise came with the sudden realisation that oil had the potential to release Scotland from the economic ties that bound it to England. The SNP exploited that in the deceptively simple slogan, 'It's Scotland's Oil'. Legally and jurisdictionally, of course, it wasn't, but the SNP was making a political point that it ought to be. In the 1960s, the SNP was a minor political player getting less than 5%; a decade later it was Scotland's second party with 30% of the vote in the October 1974 British general election, and a serious challenger to Labour. This transformed party politics in Scotland such that the main competition was established between Labour and the SNP. The erstwhile challengers, the Scottish Conservative and Unionist party, Scotland's oldest political party, went into steady then precipitate decline. Mrs Thatcher's triumphant hegemony from 1979 was an English phenomenon, and emphatically not a Scottish one. This consummate politician had no feel for Scotland, and her attacks on the public sector and on nationalised industries such as coal and steel were interpreted as an attack on Scotland itself. Labour and the SNP outbid each other in claims for the Scottish mantle, and if anything it was Labour rather than the SNP which prospered electorally in the dark winter of the 1980s. In the 1979 referendum debacle a majority of voters in Scotland had said yes to a devolved assembly, but in insufficient numbers to satisfy electoral conditions for constitutional change to happen.

Being offered an assembly, and having hopes dashed in this way, led to the long campaign first for an 'assembly', and then as confidence returned, for a 'parliament', a law-making body with more substantial powers. In 1979, the Scottish middle classes had been neutral to negative about devolution, and a majority voted against, with only 40% in favour. Eighteen years later, in the second referendum, they swung behind Home Rule, with 70% voting yes. Scotland's working class had always been in favour, and over 90% of them voted yes in the 1997 referendum. What shifted bourgeois opinion in Scotland was the steady erosion of their power over civil institutions by the Thatcher government, paradoxically in favour of powerful markets and strong state. The autonomy which the Scots had over law, education, welfare and social governance was pushed aside by a government in London who tried to ride the twin horses of neo-liberalism with regard to economic policy, and social conservatism on moral and social issues.

By the early 1990s, expectations that there would be a change of London government were dashed, and with it prospects for devolution. The language of the 'democratic deficit' entered the political lexicon. Scotland's votes counted for little in a Westminster parliament dominated by English votes; the latter were after all 85% of the UK's population. 1997 saw the nadir of Conservative fortunes in Scotland when, with 17.5% of the popular vote, they won no seats at all, the first wipe-out in their history north of the border.

This political revolution led some to the view that the collapse of Conservative support in Scotland was because Scotland was 'naturally' more left-wing than England, and on the face of it this looked plausible given that Conservatives did better in all parts of England than they did in Scotland (and Wales) even where the social and class structures of different regions were comparable. Thus, while northern England had a socio-economic profile quite similar to Scotland's, Conservatives did twice as well electorally as they did north of the border. Might there be a significant difference in social and political values? The answer is complex and revealing. Mrs Thatcher was elected in England, *despite*, not because of, English social and political values. The annual series of British Social Attitudes surveys showed unequivocally that what might be called social democratic values – belief in state intervention, income redistribution, high social spending rather than low taxation – held north *and* south of the border. There is little evidence that public opinion in the UK at large has shifted significantly to the right in the last thirty years.[9] Scotland was no exception to that. What does seem to have happened, however, is that social democratic values in Scotland have been badged as 'Scottish' just as they are thought of as 'British' in England. In other words, people who have left-of-centre values in the two countries express different national identities. This should not really surprise us, for public opinion in most late capitalist western societies moves along roughly the same lines, and it is broadly centre or left-of-centre. Precisely because the main party competition was between Labour and the SNP, both social democratic in ethos, rather than, as in England, between Labour and Tories – left versus right – the Scottish political agenda took a distinctive course.

The Scottish Frame of Reference
The key to understanding this process in Scotland however is that there such values were refracted differently than they were in England, not that there was a significant difference in the values themselves. If we divide public opinion in Scotland and England into left, centre and right in ideological terms, the Scottish 'centre' more resembles the left than it does the right.[10] How people construe their national identity makes a difference. Thus, people who are predominantly Scottish (opting for 'Scottish not British' or 'more Scottish than British') are 75% on the left, 70% in the centre, and 56% on the right. In England on the other hand the corresponding proportions – prioritising English over British – are 36% on the left, 32% in the centre and 31% on the right. As Lindsay Paterson observed: 'Governing from the centre in Scotland signifies Scottishness, and indeed attempting to govern with a British accent would tend to be interpreted as being associated with the right'.[11]

What this means is that the 'frame of reference' is the key, not that there is a set of 'objective' differences between Scotland and England either with regard to social structure or to social and political values. We search in vain for the touchstone of underlying difference. Instead, difference lies in how these structures and processes and values are interpreted. The Scottish frame of reference was, in truth, always a powerful means for refracting wider and shared processes. The skill of political parties was, and is, to act as a bridge between Scottish and British levels of governance. The Scottish electorate has grown used to exploiting its vote at British elections to defend Scottish interests, and to send a message to Westminster that it ignores Scotland at its peril. In short, it sends a signal to the political classes that if they do not accord Scotland sufficient attention then the Union – that marriage of convenience – might be at an end. This does not mean voting for the Scottish National Party as the only or best vehicle to deliver Scottish interests. In many ways, after 1979, Labour in Scotland took on that mantle, or had it thrust upon it. If anything, the SNP was an *effect* of this Scottification process, not its cause. Social and economic change are thereby interpreted through Scottish spectacles (just as similar processes will be interpreted in 'Danish' ways).

Given that the Scottish edifice of governance is substantial and elaborate, and long embedded in Scottish life, then interpreting and managing change is its *raison d'être*. We can refer to this as a political-cultural prism which, if anything, has grown rather than diminished in the last thirty years. The proactive role of Scottish 'government' in helping to restructure economic life, the discovery and impact of North Sea Oil, the rise of the SNP, the rejection of the Conservative party north of the border, have all played their part in setting up a cultural apparatus for making sense of social change in Scotland. Along the way, Westminster governments have had to adapt. Even at the height of Thatcherism in the 1980s when Conservative politicians ran the Scottish Office as the appointees of London, they played the role of 'governor-general' at their peril, and the more astute sought to ameliorate the worst impact of government policies on Scotland. In a final act of appeasement (which failed) in the mid-1990s, the neo-liberal Secretary of State for Scotland, Michael Forsyth, brought the so-called Stone of Destiny, which had been taken to London as a war trophy by the English King 800 years before, back to Scotland. Forsyth possibly hoped to reap a political return for such a 'nationalist' act but the Scottish electorate rewarded his party in 1997 by voting out every single Conservative MP. Political magic of this sort only works if the audience is willing to believe. It didn't.

Nowadays there is another set of stones on which to confer political magic: the Scottish parliament. The major political story of Scotland in the last decade has been the return of a legislature to Scotland, the first since 1707. It is, of course, a devolved not an independent parliament, but it is hard to underplay its significance. That there was 'devolution' (a Westminster word to indicate that power devolved is power retained; I give you responsibility to carry out my wishes, but I retain authority) resulted from the election of a Labour government in 1997 whose first act it was. This was 'unfinished business' in the words of the late John Smith, Labour's leader who died in opposition, and whose task it had been to steer through the first Scotland bill in the late 1970s. The task of seeing a new Scotland Act on the Statute Book in 1998 fell to Smith's fellow Glaswegian lawyer Donald Dewar, himself tragically to die while in office in 2000. Dewar's commitment to Home Rule (to use an old 19th century Liberal term to signify self-government) was whole-hearted, unlike some of his UK cabinet colleagues, and reputedly the prime minister, Tony Blair. Nevertheless, the parliament quickly became a central feature of Scottish political and social life. Its spiralling costs, its capacity to act as a lightning conductor for Scottish ills, people's expectations that it would make life better, all raised its profile. In truth, the parliament simply became another brick in the wall of Scottish social and political life.

It is, by definition, a political institution, but it is also a social and cultural one. It is not the only one which matters; after all, Scottish politics indubitably went on before there was a parliament; the parliament is a necessary institution in Scottish political life, but not sufficient in and of itself to be the only bearer of Scottish distinctiveness. In all modern societies the distinction between 'political' and 'social', between 'parliament' and 'society' is, in any case, a slippery one. Politics covers most aspects of social life these days, and civil society demands that the political process takes its concerns and problems on board in the expectation, frequently dashed, that politicians can solve them. Politicians may, as they say, be bastards; but in the Scottish case they are *our* bastards.

The Future of Scotland
What does all this mean for the future of the Union, this year marking for good or ill or both its 300th anniversary? In the rather curious and semi-detached constitutional system which is the British state, unwritten, muddling through, making it up as you go along, it is impossible to predict what will happen. Scotland is indubitably a nation, an imagined community to which most Scots give support and allegiance, while not at present wishing to leave the Union. In this curious marriage of convenience, devolution has majority support, but those wishing for independence number between 35-40%.

If devolution was a device to see off separation, then it has failed. If devolution was the thin end of the wedge to Scottish independence then, at least in the short-term, it has failed too. There are some nice disparities in people's views. Most think Westminster *is* by far the more influential institution, but also think that Holyrood *should* be the more influential parliament. Those who think things have got better with regard to education, health care and general economic well-being credit the *Scottish* institutions, and those who are pessimistic in these regards blame Westminster. In truth, devolution has had something of a mixed report card. It has high profile achievements such as free personal care for the elderly; but lax arrangements to ensure that local authorities actually carry out the policy: a ban on smoking in public places (following Ireland); but inadequate resources to help people kick the habit: land reform enabling the return of land to local communities; but an unwillingness to take on recalcitrant landlords who restrict access to land. Too often, Scottish members of parliament behave like their counterparts elsewhere; limited in vision, obsessed with the party line, willing to sound ridiculous in public because the party brief requires it. The system of proportional representation means that no party has overall control, especially on a minority of votes; but party politicians seem unwilling to deviate from the party line as ministerial advancement depends on staying close to policy.

Back in the 1980s and 1990s, the debate centred on what devolution might lead to. For the Conservatives it was the 'slippery slope' to full independence. For the SNP, it was the thin end of the wedge; the stepping stone to independence. In the early days of devolution, much public opinion thought that, whichever metaphor one used, ultimately it would have a bearing on future constitutional change. By mid-decade of the new century, most people do not think that devolution will actually lead to independence, but are fairly relaxed if, one day, it comes to pass. The vast majority of Scots think of themselves first and foremost as Scottish rather than British, but even those who deny that they are British, do not take a negative view of what British means. As many of 30% of SNP supporters do not want Independence (two-thirds do), and more Conservatives favour devolution (37%) than want the parliament abolished (33%), despite the long and unsuccessful battle their party fought during the 1980s and 1990s. Fully one-third of Labour supporters want Independence. Perhaps the way to think of these things is not in terms of a battle of absolutes, a struggle to fit people into categories ('you are a nationalist, therefore you vote for independence'), but to accept the fluidity and processual nature of political and social change. Political parties may hitch stars to constitutional options: Labour to devolution; Liberals to federalism; Nationalists to independence, but we have instead to think of these less as competing categories and more as points on a continuum of self-government.

Will the Union hold? It depends what we mean. 'The Union' is an icon, negative to some, positive to others. What it is not in any meaningful sense is the pre-democratic deal struck between two political elites, Scottish and English, three hundred years ago. What we have today would be unrecognisable to them. Scotland (and England) are not at all what they were. The Union is a flexible instrument which has withstood war and radical reform. Not having a written constitution for the UK is both good and bad. It gives central government too much power over the citizen without even bothering to ask its permission. On the other hand, it can cope with constitutional change without getting snarled up in legal niceties and political stasis. Will Scotland find sufficient reason to stay in the Union? Time, as always, will tell.

Notes

[1] Benedict Anderson, *Imagined Communities: Reflections on the Origin and Spread of*

Nationalism (London: Verso 1996)
2. Pierre Bourdieu, *Outline of a Theory of Practice* (Cambridge University Press 1977)
3. U. Østergård, 'Peasants and Danes: the Danish Nationality and Political Culture', in *Comparative Studies in Society and History*, 1992 34 (1)
4. Since 1999, a number of scholars have been engaged in a series of studies of national identities in Scotland and England, funded by the Leverhulme Trust. The results can be found at http://www.institute-of-governance.org/forum/Leverhulme/TOC.html
5. Scottish Social Attitudes survey 2005
6. The survey data in this article are taken from the Scottish Social Attitudes surveys, details of which can be found at http://www.scotcen.org.uk/
7. Asifa Hussain and William Miller, *Multicultural Nationalism: Islamophobia, Anglophobia and Devolution* (Oxford University Press 2006)
8. A fuller account of these economic, social and political processes can be found in D. McCrone *Understanding Scotland: the sociology of a nation* (London: Routledge 2001)
9. See Alison Park and Paula Surridge, 'Charting changes in British values', in *British Social Attitudes, the 20th Report: continuity and change over two decades* (London: Sage 2003)
10. Lindsay Paterson, 'Social Capital and Political Ideology', in J. Curtice, D. McCrone, A. Park and L. Paterson (eds), *New Scotland, New Society?* (Edinburgh: Polygon 2002).
11. *Ibid*, p. 212

UNION AND IDENTITY: SCOTLAND IN A SOCIAL AND INSTITUTIONAL CONTEXT

Steve Murdoch and J.R. Young

Abstract

In this essay we look from a Scottish perspective to the institutional background that facilitated this union of 1707 and its cultural consequences. Particularly, we will examine reception by the populace as evidenced through self-identification with the new structures, be they the British Monarchy, Cromwellian Commonwealth or British Parliament. This essay traces the three Anglo-Scottish unions (1603, 1654 and 1707) and discusses the impact they had on issues of institutional and cultural identity both at the time of the union of 1707 and subsequently.

1707 was a pivotal year for Scottish and English history: two independent states with fully operational governmental institutions (parliaments, privy councils, law courts, etc) decide to merge together to form a new unitary state called Great Britain. There was no conquest of one nation by the other, but rather a majority agreement in both parliaments that a full political union, representing the loss of independence for both countries, was the best solution to the variety of problems facing each country. To some it was the natural conclusion of a century of partial union through the dynastic links that placed the Scottish royal House of Stuart at the head of both kingdoms. To others, in both kingdoms, it reflected an unwarranted surrender of national sovereignty for short-term political gains. In this essay we look at the institutional background that facilitated this union from a Scottish perspective, and at some of the cultural consequences that resulted from it. The very idea of Britain had been around long before 1707, and there already existed a complex layering of identities.[1] This, therefore is not an essay about one union, but three: 1603, 1654 and 1707.

Institutional identity under the dynastic union, 1603-1707

Towards the end of the sixteenth century it became apparent that Elizabeth I of England would die childless and that she would be succeeded by James VI of Scotland. The resulting multiple-monarchy would leave James in charge of three kingdoms – Scotland, England and Ireland. Monarchs of multiple kingdoms were not an uncommon phenomenon in Europe in the sixteenth century. Scandinavia entered the century unified under the Kalmar Union. By the end of the century Sigismund Vasa found himself the monarch of the complex Polish-Lithuanian Commonwealth *and* monarch of the ex-Kalmar kingdom of Sweden. However, both the Kalmar Union and Sigismund Vasa's trans-Baltic empire eventually faltered. In the case of the Kalmar Union this was due to the resentment caused by the domination of one kingdom (Denmark) over another (Sweden). This resulted in rebellion and ultimately the independence of Sweden from the union. When dynastic providence then led to Sweden sharing her monarch with Poland-Lithuania, another rebellion followed to oust Sigismund on the basis of his Catholic religion. Personal multiple monarchies, it seems, did not always work, particularly where strong ethnic or religious factors played a role.

The populations of Britain were not unaware of these developments, indeed discussions relating to them were common. In 1604 there were numerous discourses on such unions, including those between Wales and England; Navarre and Aragon with Castile; Spain and Portugal; Normandy and Brittany with France, and Lithuania with Poland.[2] The latter was of special importance as none of the other unions 'were attended with any change of laws, excepting that of Lithuania with Poland'.[3] The various forms of union were discussed; there emerged three main types: marriage, election and conquest.[4] The complexities of this in a northern European context were revealed in one tract that noted the following;

> The kingdoms of Poleland, Hungarie, Boheme, as also Dennemarke and Sweden hath been oftentimes confused in the person of one prince by election: Poleland and Hungarie in the person of Loys, King of Hungarie by birth and of Poleland by election: Poleland and Sweden in Sigismunde now reigning: Boheme, Hungarie and Austrish in Ferdinande, late Emperour: Denmarke and Sweden in the persons of Margarette, daughter to Waldemar, Chrisierne the I and John the I.[5]

The dynastic union of 1603 met with very little resistance, even though James was unable to achieve his 'perfect union' that would have also united the Parliaments of the two nations. Thus, in the aftermath of 1603, the key institutions of Scottish government such as Parliament, Privy Council and the Law Courts remained the same. Less certain was the status of the Church of Scotland (the Kirk). Tension over the nature of the Kirk spilled over from the pre-1603 period in terms of the king's clashes with the Scottish Presbyterians and his preference for Episcopal church government. Difficulties in securing and enforcing the unpopular 'Five Articles of Perth' of 1617, either in the Kirk's General Assembly or the 1621 Parliament, marked the point beyond which James would not go in terms of ecclesiastical and liturgical reform. In the immediate post-union years, James relied on his own knowledge of Scottish affairs, the use of key advisors, and his Privy Council to aid him with the government of Scotland.[6] His Parliament, however, tended to meet less often than it had done before 1603. In the thirty-six years from 1567 to 1603 sixteen parliaments and conventions of estates were held under James VI, whereas in the twenty-two years from 1603 to the accession of Charles I in 1625 (after James' death), only seven Parliaments and eight Conventions of Estates were held.[7] In terms of the management of Scottish Parliaments on behalf of the crown, the standing committee of the 'Lords of the Articles' proved controversial in driving through unpopular policies, both in the 1621 Parliament under James VI and again in the 1633 Parliament under Charles I. It was in the reign of Charles I, however, that the negative effects of absentee monarchy, arrogant Anglocentricism and issues of British religious uniformity became particularly acute. There were now real fears that the ancient kingdom of Scotland was being reduced to the status of a province, and this resulted in the emergence of the Presbyterian Covenanting movement. These Covenanters ultimately took control of the apparatus of state power – both Parliament and Church - and played a leading role in the subsequent 'Wars for the Three Kingdoms' of 1638-1651.[8] The movement began by drafting the National Covenant, which gave them both a name and an ideological base. In addition to emphasising an unconditional covenanted relationship between the Scottish people and God, it advocated a conditional relationship with the monarchy (the people were obliged to resist a monarch who broke this covenant), and a demand for free general assemblies and parliaments without royal interference was also articulated.[9]

Charles I failed to suppress the Covenanters militarily during the Bishops' Wars (1639-40) and indeed lost two separate rounds to them in the conflict. In constitutional terms a settlement was enacted in the Covenanting Parliament of 1639-41 that enhanced the powers of the Scottish Parliament at the expense of the royal prerogative of Charles I. Parliament secured control over executive and judicial appointments, parliaments were to be held every three years and the controversial 'Lords of the Articles' were abolished. Parliament thereafter met on a regular basis between 1639 and 1651 and a vibrant committee structure existed to support it. The Privy Council had a more marginal role during these years, with Covenanting rule focused on Parliament and its committees.[10] Furthermore, episcopacy was overturned in the Kirk, which then implemented a Presbyterian structure of church government. The General Assembly met on an annual basis and its executive committee, the Commission of the Kirk, looked after church affairs when the Assembly was not in session. Close liaisons also existed between Parliament and the Kirk in terms of Covenanting government of the country and participation in the wider aspect of the British Civil Wars.[11] The Covenanters also envisaged a strong Covenanting identity not only within a British framework, but also within a European one by seeking a federal or confederal union with several European powers. First and foremost, the Covenanters wanted a Covenanted monarchy and a three-kingdom Covenanted Britain. Federalist and confederalist tendencies can be identified in 1640-41, 1643-44, 1646 and 1648. The Solemn League and Covenant of 1643, with the dream of Presbyterianism in England and Ireland, as well as Scotland, was the price demanded by the Covenanters for their supportive intervention to the English Parliament against Charles I in the English Civil War.[12] In 1644 the Covenanters also sought to extend the Solemn League and Covenant to a confederal union to include the Dutch and the Swedes as a Protestant defensive league in the ongoing Thirty Years' War.[13] However, with the Scottish population drained by continued participation in conflicts in England, Ireland and continental Europe, coupled with civil war and a *coup d'état* in Scotland, the British Civil Wars ultimately resulted in the Cromwellian conquest of Scotland by 1651. This in turn can be traced to key events in 1649, which are also important in terms of a perceived Covenanting British identity.

In the aftermath of the execution of Charles I as King of England in January 1649, the Scottish Parliament proclaimed Charles II as King of Great Britain, France and Ireland. The response of the radical godly Covenanting regime then in power was therefore to resurrect the Union of the Crowns and the monarchy on a British basis at the point when England, under Cromwell's rule, was in the process of abolishing the monarchy and becoming a republic. For the Covenanters, however, the dream of a covenanted king of the three kingdoms remained. Indeed, the admission of Charles II into the office of King of Great Britain, France and Ireland was not to be unconditional. The Parliamentary proclamation of 5 February 1649 declared him as king on a pan-British basis, but the 'Act anent Securing of Religion and Peace of the Kingdom' of 7 February 1649 laid down the terms and conditions that he would have to meet before he could actually be crowned. Charles had to subscribe to the National Covenant and the Solemn League and Covenant, which he further had to undertake to re-impose on England and Ireland. Such actions were clearly at the forefront of the explanation for the Cromwellian conquest of Scotland in 1650-1. The Anglo-Scottish war of the godly witnessed the triumph of English Cromwellian republicanism over

Scottish Covenanting unionism, and subsequently resulted in the incorporation of Scotland (and also Ireland) into the English Commonwealth and, later, Protectorate.[14]

Incorporation had been firmly on the English agenda in the aftermath of their 1651 conquest of Scotland, though it was not simple annexation (as had previously occurred in Wales). The *'Declaration of the Parliament of the Commonwealth of England, concerning the Settlement of Scotland'* of December 1651 stated that 'Scotland shall, and may be incorporated into, and become one Common-wealth with this of England'.[15] The English Parliament appointed commissioners to present a 'Tender of Union' to their Scottish counterparts in 1651.[16] Progress was eventually made in 1653 when allowance was made for 30 Scottish politicians to sit in the Commonwealth Parliament in London.[17] Soon after, on 12 April 1654, an ordinance was issued which allowed for a proper Union of England and Scotland at an institutional level. This occurred because Cromwell, now Lord Protector, had taken into consideration 'how much it might conduce to the glory of God and the peace and welfare of the people in this whole island, that after all those late unhappy wars and differences, the people of Scotland should be united with the people of England into one Commonwealth and under one Government'.[18]

The 1654 'Ordinance of Union' came down hard on traditional features of Scotland's institutional identity. The Saltire (the cross of St Andrew) was to become part of the Arms of the Commonwealth as a single 'badge' of union. All the public seals, seals of public office, and the seals of civil or corporate bodies in Scotland that formerly carried the Saltire were now to be replaced by the new 'Arms of the Commonwealth'. Furthermore, the right of the Scottish Parliament and Estates to assemble was banned as a way of emphasising the dominance of the new British institution based at Westminster. The 1654 Ordinance did not formally become an Act of Union until 1657 when it was approved by the second Protectorate Parliament.[19] From a different institutional perspective, ideological divisions within the Kirk continued throughout the early 1650s with the General Assembly last meeting in 1653. Crucially, it did not meet again until 1690, when the re-establishment of a Presbyterian church formed part of the Revolution settlement.[20] This was not least due to the return of Charles II to his British thrones in 1660.

The Restoration of the Stuart monarchy in the British Isles witnessed the abandonment of the Cromwellian Union and a return to the Union of the Crowns as *per* 1603, with two separate British kingdoms and governments under a single monarch.[21] The institutions of Scottish government returned:

its parliament, privy council and the law courts were all re-established (along with the much despised 'Lords of the Articles'). The royal prerogative was fully re-established in the Restoration settlement of 1661-3 and the Covenanting revolution was repealed along with all legislation passed by the Covenanting regime.[22] The settlement itself arguably had absolutist tendencies and should be viewed in a northern European context with regard to the legislation passed by the Estates General of Denmark-Norway in 1660, which introduced absolutism to those kingdoms.[23] In terms of religious structures, however, episcopacy was re-introduced into the Kirk, albeit religious dissent and rebellion proved to be a perennial problem for the Stuart monarchs throughout the Restoration period. Despite strong opposition from within, the Kirk remained an Episcopalian institution until the Revolution of 1689-90.[24]

Notwithstanding the bitter taste left by the Cromwellian occupation of Scotland, Anglo-Scottish unionist projects were discussed at several points during the Restoration period. Of particular note were the abortive attempts to secure an economic union. This should be viewed within the wider European context of commercial treaties, as opposed to confessional or directly political ones. The negotiators from both sides could draw on numerous examples of such pacts, including the commercial treaty between England and Denmark of 1654 (reworked as Great Britain and Denmark in 1661) which stated on the opening line that the treaty was one of 'pacis, unionis et confoederationis'.[25] The ongoing British negotiations stalled over vested protectionist interests and fears on both sides, but by 1670 the agenda had moved towards negotiations for another incorporating union. The proposed union envisaged a united parliament, free trade, commercial integration and fiscal equivalence. In terms of the theme of institutional identities, however, the two legal systems and churches were to remain separate. Within the context of an incorporating union and a single parliament, Scotland was to be represented by thirty members in the House of Commons and ten peers and two bishops in the House of Lords.[26] Thus, there are striking similarities to both the Cromwellian precedent and the successfully negotiated union enacted in 1707.[27] The 1670 negotiations faltered, not least due to the role of John Maitland, 1st Duke of Lauderdale. His insistence on legal and ecclesiastical autonomy for Scotland not only created problems in themselves, but his insistence that there be equal representation in a joint British parliament ultimately ended the negotiations.[28] It took a further twenty years before serious discussion of political union resurfaced.

In Scotland, the Revolution settlement of 1689-90 reasserted the political and constitutional power of the Scottish Estates and harked back to the Covenanting settlement of 1640-1. The 1689 'Claim of Right' forfeited James VII as King of Scotland while the notion of a limited and contractual monarchy was emphasised for his successor. Institutional change followed, the controversial 'Lords of the Articles' being, once again, abolished as part of the Presbyterian settlement. Further, 'divine-right' monarchy, as envisaged by James VI in the early seventeenth century, was rejected. The concept had only recently been reiterated under the 1681 'Hereditary Succession Act'. The absolutist leanings outlined within this act were comparable with the similar succession acts passed in 1661 in Denmark and in the Swedish *Riksdag* of 1680.[29] Once more, the Scottish establishment was fully aware of the consequences of such legislation. Thus, this act, along with the terms relating to the succession of the Catholic James, Duke of York, and the additional absolutist intentions articulated in the 1685 'Excise Act', were all fully rejected at the Scottish Revolution of 1689.[30] Commissioners were appointed by a revolutionary Convention of Estates (thereafter turned into a full Parliament by King William) to treat for union with England.[31] Although negotiations were never begun, new research has shown that many of those individuals who were responsible for securing union in 1707 had been keen on such a union in 1689. Accordingly, this new line of research argues that the direct origins of the 1707 union, and many of the key individuals involved in it, can be traced back to the Revolution when they decided that a full union was the best way forward for Scotland.[32] The 1689 Revolution also facilitated further institutional change by allowing the Kirk to reinvent itself once more. The Episcopal structure, in operation since the 1660 Restoration, was abolished and Presbyterianism was reintroduced; General Assemblies were held on an annual basis thereafter. These played an important role in the life of the nation both before and after 1707.

With both church and government structures thus secured, and a willingness by many of the establishment to bring about closer union, the process ought to have run smoothly thereafter. Yet that was not to be; Scotland under William and Mary witnessed an increased degree of Court influence in political life, and that interference was deeply resented. This was coupled with a series of actions and events that left a bitter taste in the mouths of many Scots: the 1692 Massacre of Glencoe; perceived political sabotage on the part of the monarchy, the English Parliament, and the English East India Company for the failure of the Darien project of the 1690s; Scottish involvement in European warfare; and a series of major famines. These not only created domestic problems in Scotland, but also increased tensions in Anglo-Scottish relations. Such tensions were reflected in the difficulty of managing an increasingly truculent Scottish parliament. Prior to his accidental death in 1702, William was advocating a union to resolve these problems. The new monarch, Queen Anne, was fundamentally committed to the idea of an 'entire' union. Negotiations took place in 1702-3 between parliamentary commissioners from both countries; these stalled, mainly over compensation for the Darien project and the Company of Scotland. A new parliament sat in Scotland between 1703 and 1707. The sessions of 1703-4 had a distinctly nationalist tone with Parliament asserting the right to dictate an independent foreign policy (the Act anent Peace and War) and an independent dynastic policy (the Act of Security). This was particularly sensitive, if not aggressive, vis-à-vis the Court-dominated interest and the monarch in London in the light of the ongoing War of the Spanish Succession and the 1701 English 'Act of Settlement', which provided for the Hanoverian Succession should Queen Anne die without heirs (as was likely). Faced with a hostile response in the English 'Aliens Act' of 1705 that stated that Scots would be treated as aliens in England and Scottish exports would be banned from England if the Hanoverian Succession was not approved or commissioners appointed to treat for union by Christmas Day 1705, the 1705 Scottish parliamentary session took the controversial decision to allow Queen Anne to appoint Scottish commissioners to negotiate a treaty of union with their English counterparts. Deliberations accordingly took place in 1706 and the negotiated treaty of twenty-five articles was thereafter approved and ratified firstly by the Scottish parliament and then its English counterpart. As the commissioners were appointed by the Queen, all bar one of the Scottish commissioners, George Lockhart of Carnwath, was in favour of an 'entire' union or union of incorporation; this was achieved in January 1707, leading to the creation of the unitary state of Great Britain.[33]

The treaty itself consisted of twenty-five articles, 15 of which (60%) were concerned with economic issues. Scotland was granted free trade with England and her colonies, and protectionist measures were included for key Scottish industries and sectors. The first three articles of the treaty were the most important ones. Article one stated that the two kingdoms of Scotland and England were to be united into one kingdom called Great Britain. The crosses of St Andrew and St George were to be conjoined in a manner thought fit by Queen Anne and these were to be used in all flags, banners, standards and ensigns at sea and on land. Article two provided for the Hanoverian succession in the future aftermath of Queen Anne's death, and article three stated that the united kingdom of Great Britain was to be represented by a single parliament, the parliament of Great Britain. Article twenty-two provided for Scottish representation in that parliament, with sixteen elected peers in the House of Lords and forty-five Members of Parliament in the House of Commons.[34]

Despite being an 'entire' union, however, this did not imply complete integration. Scotland maintained its distinct legal, educational and religious identity with institutions in place to support each facet. Religion was a critical area; the 1705 act of the Scottish Parliament appointing commissioners to treat for union explicitly prohibited the commissioners from discussing religion and this was not dealt with in the negotiations. When the negotiated treaty itself was made public, the Kirk and its ministers were vocal opponents of it, fearful of being submerged by Anglicanism in a British State. Legislation of 12 November 1706 secured the rights of the Presbyterian Kirk and this did much to abate opposition to the union from Scotland's premier religious institution.[35] The 1706 treaty was ratified by the Scottish parliament on 16 January 1707. The 'Church Act' was inserted in the treaty and also ratified on the same date. The Act for Securing the Protestant Religion and Presbyterian Church Government stated that the Presbyterian government of the Kirk 'shall remain and continue unalterable, And that the said Presbyterian Government shall be the only Government of the Church within the Kingdom of Scotland'. Furthermore, Scotland retained its own system of private law and law courts, while the universities and colleges of St Andrews, Glasgow, Aberdeen and Edinburgh 'now established by Law shall continue within this kingdom for ever'. Crucially, the act concluded that 'this Act of Parliament with the Establishment therein contained shall be held and observed in all time *coming* as a fundamental and essential condition of any Treaty of Union to be concluded betwixt the two kingdoms without any alteration thereof or derogation thereto in any sort for ever'.[36] In ratifying the Treaty of Union and agreeing to the abolition of the Scottish Parliament, that institution itself viewed a Presbyterian Church of Scotland, in all time coming, as a fundamental aspect of the infrastructure and identity of a post-1707 Scotland within a British state. Indeed, the church, the law and the education system were the key ingredients of civic Scottish society in the post-1707 period and had a profound impact on Scotland's post-Union identity. As noted by William Ferguson, the union of 1707 'produced a new state and went some way towards creating a new quasi-national consciousness, but at the same time the union preserved two ancient national entities. It was in essence a union of states, not of nations'.[37] Two national churches were enshrined in the British Union, with the curious situation of the Anglican bishops in the House of Lords being sworn to uphold Presbyterianism throughout 'North Britain'.

Cultural identity under the Dynastic Union

Too often history is related as the history of dynasties and institutions without notice being taken of how dynastic change and institutional development impacted on the people who lived under such structures. In Britain in the period following the dynastic union of 1603 there were strong attempts made to try to mirror the constitutional developments by re-aligning cultural and social identities to better fit the realities brought about by the Stuart succession in England. In 1604 King James had asked if he might use the title of 'King of Great Britain' without detriment to the kingdoms of Scotland or England.[38] It was not long before an ethnic identity began to attach itself to the new institutionally 'British' monarchy. In 1594 the term *Scoti-Britannorvm* had been used by Andrew Melville to celebrate the birth of Prince Henry Stuart, perhaps in anticipation of the Union of Crowns.[39] The innovation of a Scottish-British identity did not take long to catch on, particularly among those trying to impress their royal masters at Court. The essayist Alexander Craig published his poetical collection of essays in 1604 adding *Scoto-Britane* after his name.[40] David Hume of Godscroft published his *De Unione Insulae Britannicae* which went further in defining exactly what Britain should mean.[41] These men published their works during the union debates of 1604-1607, which King James had hoped would end in full Parliamentary union between the two nations - and thus the Scottish-British appellation is understandable. From the Jacobean period onwards many Scots were found both publicly and privately calling themselves British, such as John Gordon, who published his work with the identifier of *Scoto-Britannem* in 1612 and also matriculated in Leiden in October the same year as *Scot-Britannus*.[42] Archibald Stephens gained a medical degree at Leiden University on 16 July 1661 and was recorded in the matriculation records as '*Scoto-Brit*', as were his countrymen Gilbert Rule in 1665 and John Galloway in 1675.[43] In 1682, Robert Sinclair matriculated as '*Scoto-Britannus*' in Utrecht, as did George Flaminius in 1689.[44] They were followed by David Plenderleith, a Scot registered at Frankfurt-an-der-Oder in 1699 as '*nobilis Scoto-Brittanus*'.[45] Examples of the Scoto-Briton abound both in the public sphere, as evidenced in published works, and in private demonstrations of Scoto-Britishness as seen in the matriculation records. This approval granted by individuals from different levels of society was not confined to the Scots.

There has been an assumption that 'British' in the post-1603 period was something pushed on the English, who rejected it as a Scottish innovation, and who historically 'have steadfastly refused to be anything other than English'.[46] Michael Lynch has further stated that the 1640s represented a time 'when Scots (but not the English) could talk of themselves as British subjects'.[47] However, a perusal of seventeenth-century published sources reveals that a number of Englishmen styled themselves '*Anglo-Britannus*' in this period. John Price (c.1602-1676) penned poetry for Anna of Denmark and, in seeking royal patronage, may have simply adopted the British style to please King James.[48] The Earl of Nottingham wrote to Christian IV in his capacity of English High Admiral, signing his letter to the Danish king as '*Anglo-Britannus*'.[49] Similarly to the Scottish examples there were those who made their British declaration in private. On 8 May 1619, Josephus Micklethwaite registered at the University of Leiden and matriculated as '*Anglo-Brittanus*'.[50] Other English students matriculated in the same way in subsequent years; such as the scholar Sir George Ent in Padua in 1636.[51] The public declaration of Anglo-Britishness continued throughout the Carolinian period when Sir Henry Spelman published under the name '*Henrici Spelmanni Equit. Anglo-Brit*'.[52] Other authors also variously described themselves as *Brit-Anglo*, like James Howell in 1646, or even published journals such as *Mercurius Anglo-Britannus* in 1648.[53] In one way or another, the public declaration of Anglo-Britishness can be associated with a desire to support a concept of identity at a particular time. This found its greatest expression as English and Scottish Royalists sought to find a way of being patriotic to the cause of the House of Stuart while at the same time distancing themselves from the constitutional nationalism espoused by the two Parliaments during the British civil wars, 1639-1660. Howell's stated Britishness publicly announced his opposition to the institutionally united Parliaments signed up to the Solemn League and Covenant. The early reign of Charles II offers several further examples, with Sir Richard Fanshawe publishing an edition of *La Fida Pastoria* in 1658 under the pseudonym '*F. F. Anglo-Britannus*'. Interestingly, Anglo-Britishness was not dropped at the Stuart Restoration of 1660. In 1662, John Rogers matriculated at Utrecht and registered himself as '*Anglo-Brit*', as did William Barbour the following year.[54] John Harrison matriculated in Padua in 1665 and he too did so as '*Anglo-Britannus*'.[55] The Williamite Anglo-Britons were exemplified by 'Thomas Pope-Blount *Anglo-Britannus Baronettus*', whose book, *Censvra Celebriorvm Authorvm*, was advertised on the back of a published sermon 'preached before the Queen' on 16 July 1690.[56]

Like those Scots who bought into the concept of a single British identity, the presence of these Anglo-Britons confirms that 'British' was a concept bought into by *some* Scots and *some* Englishmen, indicative of a conceptual national identity that existed long before 1707. Crucially, 'Britishness' never appeared to catch on with the majority of the population in either kingdom, most of whom felt attached to their Scottish and English identities. Indeed for every example of self-identified Britons we uncover, we find far more examples of Scots fighting to retain and promote their identity. This is illustrated by the Scottish soldiers who enlisted in the Danish army in 1626.

> His majesty [of Denmark] would have the officers to carry the Dane's crosse, which the officers refusing, they were summoned to compeare before his majestie at Raynesberge to know the reasons of their refusals; at the meeting none would adventure, fearing his majestie's indignation, to gainestand openly his Majestie's will, being then his Majestie's sworne servants; and for the eschewing of greater inconvenience the officers desired so much time of his Majesty as to send Captain Robert Ennis into England to know his majestie of Great Britaine's will, whether or no they might carrie without reproach the Dane's Crosse in Scottish colours.[57]

Artwork by Rab Gordon, copyright Rainnea Graphics 2002

This incident illustrates that loyalty to the symbolism of Scotland, not Britain, was of great importance to these soldiers despite their presence in Denmark being a direct result of the dynastic alliance that bound the House of Stuart to the House of Oldenburg. In their own way, these officers had shown they were not the sort of malleable mercenaries Christian was recruiting elsewhere. More importantly, their example was followed soon after by a remarkable climb down from Britishness by one of the premier Scottish political institutions, the Privy Council. In 1630, the Scottish Privy Council commanded Sir John Scott, the Director of the Chancellery, to avoid the usage of the term Great Britain in treaties after the Stuart Court had advocated a common fisheries project which overrode the rights, privileges and vested interests of the Scottish landed and commercial classes.[58] Scott believed the term 'Great Britain' misrepresented Scotland and England which he argued were 'twa free and distinct estates and kingdomes and sould be differenced by thair particular names and not confoundit under the name of Great Britane'.[59] The Council continued that:

> the prejudice whiche this kingdome susteanes by suppressing the name of Scotland in all the infeftments, patents writts and records thairofe passing under his Majesteis name and confounding the same under the name of Great Britane, altho there be no unioun as yitt with England nor the style of Great Britane receaved there, bot all the public writts and records of that kingdome ar past his Majesties name as King of England, Scotland, France and Ireland; and thairfoir humblie to intreate his Majestie to give warrand to his Majesteis Counsell that all infeftments, patents, letters and writts passing herafter under his Majesteis name be conceaved under the name and style of Scotland, England, France and Ireland, defender of the faith, and that the style of Great Britane be forborne.[60]

This instruction from the Scottish Privy Council is symptomatic of a general distancing by Scottish institutions from Stuart politics, which eventually led to the Bishops' Wars and the temporary demise of the notional Stuart-British state. However, after 1707 the security gained by the Scottish establishment for its political, legal and religious institutions left the question of personal ethnic identity still quite open to interpretation.

'British' identities in the post-1707 period

Identity is a complex issue which, at some level, reacts to institutional developments such as the Union of Crowns, the British Civil Wars, or the Williamite Revolution. It was no different after that monumental constitutional realignment of 1707. Historians often imply that, after the political union, the Scots suddenly forgot their ancient identity and instead opted for a new identity of 'North British'.[61] In truth, that was simply one form of expressing Britishness which dated right back to the Union of Crowns. For example, John Douglas had been ordained as a minister of 'the Auld North-British Regiment' in the service of the Dutch Republic as early as 1606.[62] Several years later the Kent-based Scottish minister, Alexander Lumisden, defined himself as a 'North-Britane' in his published sermons in 1614.[63] Very little had changed since Jacobean times and the post-1707 North British only represented one of many manifestations of identity within Scotland. True, many of the Scottish political elite opted, at specific times, to call themselves North British. However, there is ample evidence to show that a distinctly Scottish identity remained strong, even among this same elite who occasionally flirted with notions of Britishness. As T.C. Smout has observed:

There was hardly a single articulate figure in eighteenth-century Scotland who did not at one time or another firmly, and generally approvingly, describe himself as a Scot.[64]

He is of course referring to individuals such as David Hume, Adam Smith, and Robert Burns, but also to George Gordon, Lord Byron, who famously said in later life:

But I am half a Scot by birth, and bred
A whole one, and my heart flies to my head, -
As 'Auld Lang Syne' brings Scotland one and all,
Scotch plaids, Scotch snoods, the blue hills and the clear streams,
The Dee, the Don, Balgounie Brig's black wall.[65]

Byron was born in England of mixed parentage and educated in Scotland before embarking on his Grand Tour. So his attachment to Scotland in this statement is most revealing. Being of mixed-parentage in any country in any age can result in a complex rendering of identity, particularly if you are in a state like Great Britain, where one population outnumbers the other, yet where multiple ethnicities belong to the same state. Take the case of Charlotte Ann Waldie who in 1817 wrote:

With these sentiments [about pride of country] deeply impressed upon my mind; with the proud consciousness, that highly as the fame of England had stood in all ages, she had now attained an unparalleled height of greatness and glory; [...] that her name would descend to the latest times as unrivalled in arms, invincible by land and sea, and pre-eminent, not only in valour, but in faith and honour, - in justice, mercy, and magnaminity (sic), - and in public virtue, – I returned to my country, after all the varying and eventful scenes through which it had been my lot to pass, - more proud than when I left it of the name of AN ENGLISHWOMAN.[66]

So what did it mean for this Scottish-born writer to declare so boldly that she was an Englishwoman? That is debatable, but we should not forget that Waldie's mother was English and that, publishing anonymously, she was writing for an audience composed of a much larger English readership than Scots. Nonetheless, within the text, Waldie was certainly keen to convey her Scottishness at the appropriate moment. In the same text where she refers to both the 'English' army and the 'British' army she also expresses her pride in the 'Highlanders' within that force who spoke 'broad Scotch' and of whom she wrote:

Some of them were from the Highlands and some from the Lowlands. And when they found that I came from Scotland, and lived upon the Tweed, they were quite delighted. One of them was from the Tweed as well as myself, he said 'he cam oot o Peebleshire'.[67]

Clearly Waldie, being of mixed parentage, was comfortable with her own complex identity and able to recognise the variety of regional and national affiliations of her fellow Britons with whom she met. When the opportunity arose to exploit her regional and national identity to the Scottish troops she did so, and recorded it with relish; she successfully exploited her plurality of nationality in a way many Scots had done since the Union of Crowns at the start of the seventeenth century. It is this complexity that is so often overlooked. For instance, this surfaces in the reporting of the memorable actions of the North British Dragoons, a British regiment who also called themselves the Scots Greys. At Waterloo they famously charged the French with the cry 'Scotland Forever', which has been picked up on by scholars like P.H. Scott as an event at which 'for the first time Scots also began to share patriotic feelings in common with their neighbours and old enemies across the Tweed'.[68] This is misplaced and, in fact, elements of the two nations had been sharing such conjoined attachment to the common British *patria* since the advent of the first self-defining 'Britons' of the early seventeenth-century. What the war cry of the Scots Greys *did* represent was the ability to possess both an official British title (institutional *via* their presence in the British army), and the informal Scottish one they preferred (ethnic and expressed through their own words). Thus we see that concepts of Scottishness survived after 1707, and throughout the subsequent centuries. Despite this, many scholars report Scotland as a place devoid of meaningful expressions of identity beyond North-Britishness until the rise of the home rule movement in the twentieth century.[69] Often overlooked are the frequent articulations of Scottishness by numerous individuals. Further, the attachment to Britain that was self-evident among many Scots is often taken to represent an acceptance of the supremacy of Anglo-Britishness. If only one source need be cited to challenge that assumption, none is more compelling than the '*Petition to Queen Victoria*' of 1897.[70] This document contains 104,647 signatures and extends to some three quarters of a mile in length. The crux of the document is to complain at the misuse of the term 'England' to represent 'Great Britain'. After a review of the history of the nation to 1707, the petitioners continued:

We, your Petitioners, being Scotsmen or descendants of Scotsmen, and most loyal subjects of your Majesty, respectfully [...] point out to your Most Gracious

Majesty that this general and continuous use of the terms "England" and "English" in an Imperial sense is a direct aggression on the national honour of their Country. For such usage implies that Scotland is part of, or is simply a province of England, and that Scotsmen are subjects of England. It is insulting, also, to our personal honour as Scotsmen; for it implies that so long as we obtain all the material advantages that are the result of a union between the two countries, we are of so mercenary a character that national honour is to us a matter of the greatest indifference [...].

We deem it a matter deeply to be regretted that there is no Court of Law to which we can appeal for the rectification of this constant aggression on our national rights as Scotsmen [...]. But there is no redress for your Majesty's Scottish subjects when their national honour is debased, and that of England is proportionally and unjustly exalted, by the improper use of the terms "England" and "English" in an imperial sense [...].

We fear that this constant and deliberate use of an incorrect Imperial nomenclature is due, not merely to ignorance or to carelessness, but largely to an unfair and aggressive feeling of national vanity on the part of an influential portion of the English people; which, if continued, will in course of time lead to a destruction of that feeling of British unity which for a long time contributed to the greatness and the glory of the Empire. To that greatness, and to that glory, Scotland has freely given her share, and even more than her share, in treasure, brain, and blood [...].

We may further point out to Your Most Gracious Majesty, that this unjust and unconstitutional attempt to Anglicise the United Kingdom, and to make England and Englishmen the sole representatives of a British power and of the British name, must necessarily have a most injurious effect on the all-important question of unity between Britain and Further Britain, or Britain-beyond-the-Seas [...].

To Your Most Gracious Majesty, then, as the fountain of honour in the British Empire, we appeal for the protection of our national honour as Scotsmen [...]. With confidence, therefore, we look to Your Majesty to preserve for us our constitutional rights as Scotsmen, as defined in the First Article of the Treaty of Union.

Importantly, the petitioners do not describe themselves as North British seeking redress from their South British countrymen, but throughout call themselves Scotsmen. They went on to give examples of the improper usage of language that demeaned Scotland, including Queen Victoria's own inappropriate conflation of England and Britain in speeches to the Houses of Parliament. Among those singled out by the petitioners was one from 21 January 1886 which noted that "**English** and Russian Commissioners, with the full consent of my ally, the Amir of Afghanistan, have been engaged, "

&c.[71] They followed this with examples of incorrectly worded treaties between Britain and foreign powers such as the following:

> It is understood between the High Contracting Parties, without prejudice to the express provisions of the Articles I., II., and IV. Of the Annex of 1st July, 1878, that His Imperial Majesty the Sultan, in assigning the Island of Cyprus to be occupied and administered by **England** has thereby transferred and vested in Her Majesty the Queen, &c.[72]

And the one that seemed to hurt most, as it was the one they finished their petition with, was the inscriptions to the dead:

> In Memory
> of the
> **English**, French and Russians
> who fell
> in the Battle of Inkermann,
> 5th November 1854[73]

The objections noted by the petitioners can still be raised to this day with expressions such as 'Anglo-Irish' Agreement rather than a 'British-Irish' accord being common parlance in the British media. Indeed many of the same objections raised in this nineteenth century petition would appear to rattle elements of the Scottish population today. However, without the British Empire (a key part of the document) as a unifying institution, with monarchism on the wane and secularism on the increase, there seems to be far less holding the British Union together today than the avowed Scoto-British who composed, or signed up to, this document could have imagined. What they did show was that even in times described in purely British terms by historians, a sense of distinct Scottishness existed, despite the loss of a major institution like a national Parliament to sustain it.

Concluding remarks

The years between 1603-1707 witnessed three distinct unions between Scotland and England (1603, 1654 and 1707) and a century of debate to go along with them on what the political, institutional and social direction would be for the populations of the island of Britain. The dynastic union of 1603 proved initially popular, James's subsequent reputation as a weak and unwelcome king in England only being voiced in a serious way by anti-Royalist partisans during the British Civil Wars. During his reign elements within the populace on both sides of the border were keen to show their support for his new British monarchy by publicly and privately subscribing to his notion of a single British identity. While James was alive even the institutions that sought to remain separate, the parliaments and churches, could still support 'Britishness' by adding the caveat of Anglo-British or Scoto-British to maintain their older identity while supporting the new one. When the very monarchy itself came under threat during the British Civil Wars, many Royalists who might previously have remained aloof from the *nouveau* British nationality, rallied to it as a way of advertising their support for Charles I and distancing themselves from the institutional confederal union of the Solemn League and Covenant.

As demonstrated above, however, even institutions like the Scottish Privy Council, appointed by the king, could reject Britishness when they thought that the nation they represented was threatened by usage of the term. What is perhaps too often forgotten is that institutions are composed of people and people can have multiple loyalties. These do not always reflect blind adherence to directives from higher authority as first the Scottish, and then the English, parliaments demonstrated to a monarch who tried to dictate changes to his institutions without consideration for, or consultation with, those who sat within them. Institutional challenges in church and state thus left the British populace with a number of choices with regard to the prioritising of their plural identities. The 1654 Union did not contribute to this, however, as that union was forced through military occupation, a process which has a habit of galvanising a population into rejecting any new identity being forced upon them.

Here a very interesting comparison would be to see how long a concept of Danishness lasted in the three provinces east of the Sound after they were ceded to Sweden. In the Scottish case the occupation lasted only nine years and the union less than six. Most people remembered a free Scotland and could hope the occupation would not last and, unlike for the 'East of Sound' Danes, the occupiers soon left. Furthermore, the occupiers in Scotland (like the Swedes in Skåne) had no intention of giving up their English identity to accommodate their fellow 'Commonwealthers' from Scotland and Ireland. Thus the 1654 union is distinct from 1603 and 1707 in not casting up a cultural identity to accompany it, even among those who worked for the government (not least because many Scottish seats in Parliament remained unfilled, or were occupied by Englishmen representing Scottish constituencies). However, some Scots who worked for the Commonwealth still weighted their Scottishness, such as John Durie who defiantly described himself as *Theologo Scoto-Britanno* while on a diplomatic mission to Sweden for Oliver Cromwell in 1653, thus emphasising a kind of pragmatic resistance to the

Englishing of his nation's identity.[74]

The 1707 union had far more support from the Scots than the 1654 incorporation. True, it also had vocal detractors, and anti-unionist partisans have left the most nationalistic tracts decrying the institutional change. That said, for many Scots the union sealed the Reformation of 1560 as Presbyterianism in Scotland was finally secured. Many who did not support the union were comfortably ambivalent to it given their more sincere interest in the main surviving Scottish institution – the Kirk. Thus there were those in the post-1707 period who could happily call themselves Britons or North British or Scots; the *Petition to Queen Victoria* is surely testament to the multifaceted nature of Scottish identity, which is far more complex than the simplistic attempts by those historians who have sought to confine it to 'North British' or indeed simply to 'Scottish' would allow. Three hundred years after 1707 identity in Scotland is as difficult to quantify as it always was, though undoubtedly more attention is being paid by scholars to the expressions and opinions beyond those of the political and literary elite. What is certain is that in 2007 it is a subject that still causes fierce debate.

Notes

[1] R. Mason, 'Scotland, Elizabethan England and the Idea of Britain' in *Transactions of the Royal Historical Society*, 14 (2004).

[2] *Calendar of State Papers, Domestic Series* [hereafter *CSPD*], First Series, 1547-1625 (13 vols., London, 1856-1992), vol. 1603-1610, p. 101, various tracts, 26 April 1604.

[3] *CSPD*, 1603-1610, p. 100. Discourse on Union, 26 April 1604.

[4] *CSPD*, 1603-1610, p. 100. Discourse on Union, 26 April 1604.

[5] B.R. Galloway and B.P. Levack, (eds.), *The Jacobean Union: Six Tracts of 1604* (Edinburgh 1985), p. 36

[6] See K.M. Brown, *Kingdom or Province? Scotland and the Regal Union, 1603-1715* (London 1993), pp. 1-110; M. Lee, *Government by Pen. Scotland under James VI and I* (Urbana 1980).

[7] M.D. Young, (ed.), *The Parliaments of Scotland. Burgh and Shire Commissioners* (2 vols., Edinburgh, 1992-3), volume two, pp. 753-5.

[8] See, for example, Brown, *Kingdom or Province?*, pp. 1-34; A.I. Macinnes, *Charles I and the Making of the Covenanting Movement 1625-1641* (Edinburgh 1991); A.I. Macinnes, *The British Revolution 1629-1660* (Basingstoke, 2005); D. Stevenson, *The Scottish Revolution 1637-44*, (Edinburgh 2003 edition) and *Revolution and Counter-Revolution in Scotland 1644-51* (Edinburgh 2003 edition).

[9] W.C. Dickinson & G. Donaldson, (eds.), *A Source Book of Scottish History*, volume three, 1567-1707 (Edinburgh, 1961 edition), pp. 95-104; Macinnes, *Charles I and the Making of the Covenanting Movement*; Stevenson, *The Scottish Revolution*; M. Lee, *The Road to Revolution. Scotland Under Charles I, 1625-1637* (Urbana, 1985).

[10] J.R. Young, *The Scottish Parliament 1639-1661. A Political and Constitutional Analysis* (Edinburgh, 1996), pp. 1-296; D. Stevenson, (ed.), *The Government of Scotland under the Covenanters 1637-51*, (Edinburgh, 1982).

[11] D. Stevenson, 'The General Assembly and the Commission of the Kirk, 1638-51', in D. Stevenson, (ed.), *Union, Revolution and Religion in Seventeenth-Century Scotland* (Aldershot, 1997), pp. 59-79; J.R. Young, 'The Covenanters and the Scottish Parliament, 1639-51: the Rule of the Godly and the "Second Scottish Reformation"', in E. Boran & C. Gribben, (eds.), *Enforcing Reformation in Ireland and Scotland 1500-1700* (Aldershot, 2006), pp. 131-158.

[12] A.I. Macinnes, 'Politically Reactionary Brits? The Promotion of Anglo-Scottish Union, 1603-1707', in S.J. Connolly, (ed.), *Kingdoms United? Great Britain and Ireland since 1500. Integration and Diversity* (Dublin, 1999), pp. 48-50; J. Morrill, 'Three kingdoms and one commonwealth? The enigma of mid-seventeenth century Britain and Ireland', in A. Grant & K.J. Stringer, (eds.), *Uniting the Kingdom? The Making of British History* (London, 1995), pp. 178-86; Dickinson & Donaldson, *A Source Book of Scottish History*, pp. 121-5; D. Stevenson, 'The Early Covenanters and the Federal Union of Britain', in Stevenson, *Union, Revolution and Religion*, pp. 163-81.

[13] J.R. Young, 'The Scottish Parliament and European Diplomacy 1641-1647: the Palatine, the Dutch Republic and Sweden', in S. Murdoch, (ed.), *Scotland and the Thirty Years' War 1618-1648* (Leiden, 2001), pp. 77-106; A. Grosjean, *An Unofficial Alliance: Scotland and Sweden, 1569-1654* (Leiden, 2003), pp. 200-210.

[14] See for example, Young, *The Scottish Parliament*, pp. 223-4; F.D. Dow, *Cromwellian Scotland 1651-1660* (Edinburgh, 1979).

[15] C.S. Terry, (ed.), *The Cromwellian Union 1651-1652: Papers relating to the negotiations for an incorporating union between England and Scotland, 1651-1652* (Edinburgh, 1902), p. xxii. From a Cromwellian perspective, this was to be of benefit to the people of Scotland.

[16] Terry, *The Cromwellian Union*, pp. xv-185, has the most extensive account of this process; B.P. Levack, *The Formation of the British State. England, Scotland and the Union 1603-1707* (Oxford, 1987), pp. 9-10.

[17] Terry, *The Cromwellian Union*, pp. xlviii-xlix; S.R. Gardiner, (ed.), *The Constitutional Documents of the Puritan Revolution 1625-1660* (Oxford, 1906, third edition), pp. 405-17; P.J. Pinckney, 'The Scottish representation in the Cromwellian Parliament of 1656' in *The Scottish Historical Review*, vol. xlvi, 2, no. 142 (October 1967); J.A. Casada, 'The Scottish representatives in Richard Cromwell's Parliament', *Scottish Historical Review*, vol. li, 2, no. 152 (October 1972).

[18] S.R. Gardner, (ed.), *Constitutional Documents of the Puritan Revolution, 1625-1660* (Oxford, 1899), p. 418.

[19] Gardner, *Constitutional Documents*, pp. 418-22; Terry, *The Cromwellian Union*, pp.xlix-lxxiv; A. Woolrych, *Britain in Revolution 1625-1660* (Oxford 2002), p. 572; D.L. Smith, *A History of the Modern British Isles 1603-1707* (Oxford 1998), pp. 177-9; Levack, *The Formation of the British State*, p. 10.

[20] P. Little, *Lord Broghill and the Cromwellian Union with Ireland and Scotland* (Woodbridge 2004), pp. 95-123; Dickinson & Donaldson, *A Source Book of Scottish History*, pp.

143-8, 152, 211-7.
21. Dickinson & Donaldson, *A Source Book of Scottish History*, p. 467.
22. See for example, Young, *The Scottish Parliament*, pp. 304-23.
23. J.R. Young, 'The Scottish Parliament in the Seventeenth Century: European perspectives', in A.I. Macinnes, T. Riis & F.G. Pedersen, (eds.), *Ships, Guns and Bibles in the North Sea and the Baltic States, c.1350-c.1700* (East Linton, 2000), pp. 139-72.
24. Dickinson & Donaldson, *A Source Book of Scottish History*, pp. 152-217.
25. For the Danish treaty and 'articuli pacis, unionis et confoederationis' see L. Laurensen, (ed.), *Danmark-Norges Traktater, 1523-1750: med dertil hørende aktstykker* (11 vol., Copenhagen, Nielsen & Lydiche, 1916), III, pp. 134-159. 'traktat mellem Oliver Cromwell, Protector af England og Frederik III af Danmark-Norge, 15 September 1654. For the renewed 'British' treaty see ibid., V, pp. 389-410. 'Alliance og Handelstraktat mellem Danmark-Norge og Storbritannien', 13 February 1661; Macinnes, 'Politically Reactionary Brits?', pp. 50-51.
26. Macinnes, 'Politically Reactionary Brits?, pp. 50-51; W. Ferguson, *Scotland's Relations with England: A Survey to 1707* (Edinburgh),p. 156; Macinnes, 'Politically Reactionary Brits?', p. 51. For details of the proceedings of the 1670 negotiations, see Terry, *The Cromwellian Union*, appendix, pp. 187-224.
27. Ferguson, *Scotland's Relations with England*, p. 156.
28. Ferguson, *Scotland's Relations with England*, pp. 156-7; Macinnes, 'Politically Reactionary Brits?', pp. 51-2.
29. Young, 'The Scottish Parliament in the Seventeenth Century', pp. 152-7.
30. J.R. Young, 'The Scottish Parliament and National Identity from the Union of the Crowns to the Union of the Parliaments' in D. Broun, R.J. Finlay & M. Lynch, (eds.), *Image and Identity. The Making and Re-making of Scotland Through the Ages* (Edinburgh, 1998), pp. 121-3; Young, 'The Scottish Parliament and the Covenanting heritage of constitutional reform' in A.I. Macinnes & J. Ohlmeyer, (eds.), *The Stuart Kingdoms in the Seventeenth Century* (Dublin, 2002), pp. 230-42.
31. P.W.J. Riley, *King William and the Scottish Politicians* (Edinburgh, 1979), pp. 49-53.
32. C.A. Whatley, *The Scots and the Union* (Edinburgh, 2006), pp. xiv, 29-31, 58
33. See ibid for the most recent work on these themes. See also M. Fry, *The Union. England, Scotland and the Treaty of 1707* (Edinburgh, 2006); D. Watt, *The Price of Scotland. Darien, Union and the Wealth of Nations* (Edinburgh, 2007) is now the most exhaustive study of the Darien project.
34. C. Whatley, *Bought and Sold for English Gold? Explaining the Union of 1707*, (East Linton, 2001 edition), prints the articles of the treaty on pp. 101-7.
35. See for example, *Scotland's Relations with England*, pp. 235-77.
36. Scotland, Parliament. *The Acts of the Parliaments of Scotland* (12 vols., London: 1814-1875), XI, 1702-1707, pp. 402-3.
37. Ferguson, *Scotland's Relations with England*, p.237.
38. *CSPD*, 1603-1610, pp. 96-97. King James to Cecil, 18 April 1604 and Draft reply from [the English] Parliament, 23 April 1604.
39. Andrew Melville, *Principis Scoti-Britannorum Natalia* (Edinburgh, 1594); it was

also a notion to which other Scottish poets like George Buchanan subscribed. See P.G. McGinnis and A.H. Williamson, (eds.), *George Buchanan: The Political Poetry* (Edinburgh, 2000), intro. and 'Appendix C' of that collection, p. 284: P.G. McGinnis and A.H. Williamson, (eds.), *The British Union: A critical edition and translation of David Hume of Godscroft's De Unione Insulae Britannicae* (Aldershot, 2002), p. 11.

40 A. Craig, THE POETICAL ESSAYES OF ALEXANDER CRAIGE SCOTOBRITANE. *Seene and Allowed*, (London, 1604); John Gordon, *Anti-bellarmino-torto fine Tortus Retortus ... per Ioannen Gordonivm Scotobritannem*, (London, 1612); For a general discussion of his work and the implications for 'Great Britain' see A.H. Williamson, 'Scotland, Antichrist and the invention of Great Britain' in J. Dwyer, R. Mason and A. Murdoch, (eds.), *New Perspectives on the Politics and Culture of Early Modern Scotland* (Edinburgh, 1982), p. 44.

41 McGinnis and Williamson, *The British Union*, p. 155.

42 John Gordon, *Anti-bellarmino-torto fine Tortus Retortus ... per Ioannen Gordonivm Scotobritannem* (London, 1612); For his matriculation in Leiden see *Album studiosorum academiae Lugduno Batavae*, (The Hague, 1875), 19 October 1612.

43 P.C. Molhuysen, *Bronnen tot de geschiedenis der leidsche universiteit* ('S Gravenhage, 1918), III, pp. 294, 302, 323.

44 See their various entries in *Album Studiosorum Academiae Rhenu-Traiec* (Utrecht, 1886).

45 T. Fischer, *The Scots in Germany* (Edinburgh, 1902), p. 313.

46 Dwyer, Mason and Murdoch, *New Perspectives on the Politics and Culture of Early Modern Scotland*, intro, 1.

47 M. Lynch, *Scotland: A New History*, (London, 1991), p. 317.

48 *Oxford DNB*.

49 Danish Rigsarkiv, TKUA, England AII/12. Brev fra Nottingham til Christian IV, 5 October 1616.

50 *Album studiosorum academiae Lugduno Batavae* (The Hague, 1875), 8 May 1619.

51 'English-speaking medical students attending European universities in the seventeenth century', published online by the Royal College of Physicians of Edinburgh website. Consulted 10 November 2004. See http://www.rcpe.ac.uk/library/English_Students/Padua/Padua_DtoG.html.

52 See for example H. Spelman, *Henrici Spelmanni Equit. Anglo-Brit. ARCHÆOLOGVS. In modum glossarii ad rem posteriorem &c.* (London, 1626). The volume covered obsolete words from ecclesiastical and legal vocabularies. See also *Oxford DNB*.

53 James Howell, *Angliae Suspiria ... Aut. Ia. Howell, Brit.Anglo* (London, 1646); S. Brown *Mercurius Anglo-Britannus* ('s Gravenhage, 1648).

54 *Album Studiosorum Academiae Rhenu-Traiec* (Utrecht, 1886).

55 'English-speaking medical students' as cited in note 51.

56 See the advertisement attached to G. Burnet, *A Sermon Preached before the Queen, at White-Hall, on the 16th day of July, 1690, being the monthly-fast by the Right Reverend Father in God, Gilbert Lord Burnet* (London, 1690).

57 R. Monro, *His Expedition with a worthy Scots Regiment called Mac-keyes*, (2 vols.,

London, 1637), I, p. 2. Charles I eventually gave the Scots the choice of two colours. One had a *Dannebrog* with a Saltire in the corner, the other had a Saltire with a *Dannebrog* in the corner and sketches of both were given with exact instructions for the colours of each. The comment was added that they could choose which one they wanted, but they had to choose one in order to get the King of Denmark's pay. See Public Records Office (London), SP75/8, f.61. 'The state of the King of Denmark's army', March 1627

58 Macinnes, *Charles I*, pp. 108-113.
59 Scotland, Privy Council. *Registers of the Privy Council of Scotland*, [hereafter *RPCS*] Second Series, 1625-1660 (8 vols., Edinburgh, 1899-1908), IV, pp. 56-57.
60 *RPCS*, second series, IV, pp. 56-57.
61 For discussion of North Britishness in an 18th century context see Kidd, *Subverting Scotland's Past*, particularly pp. 99, 205-215; R.J. Finlay, 'Caledonia or North Britain? Scottish identity in the Eighteenth Century' in Broun, Finlay and Lynch, *Image and Identity*, pp. 143-156. For a wider discussion on identity in Scotland see S. Murdoch, *Network North: Scottish Kin, Commercial and Covert Associations in Northern Europe, 1603-1746* (Leiden, 2006), chapters 1-3.
62 A.C. Dow, *Ministers to the Soldiers of Scotland* (Edinburgh, 1962), p. 63.
63 Alexander Lumisden, *A Heavenly Portion, Set down in Sermon, Preached at the the Funerall of Mistress Frances Sentleger, at Smeeth: in the Countie of Kent [...] By Alexander Lumisden, North-Britane, Preacher of the word of God, at Postling in Kent*, (London, 1614); Peter Hay of Naughton used 'North Britain' to describe Scotland in 1627 in his, *An Advertisment to the Subjects of Scotland, Of the fearful dangers threatned to Christian States, And namely to GREAT BRITANE, by the Ambition of Spayne [...] Also Diverse other TREATISES, touvhing the present estate of the KINGDOM of SCOTLAND [...] Written by PETER HAY, of Naughton, in NORTH-BRITANE*, (Aberdeen, 1627).
64 T.C. Smout, 'Problems of nationalism, identity and improvement in later eighteenth-century Scotland" in T.M. Devine, (ed.), *Improvement and Enlightenment* (1989), p. 5.
65 George Gordon, Lord Byron, *'Don Juan'*, Canto X, stanza XVII-XVIII.
66 D. McMillan, (ed.), *The Scotswoman at Home and Abroad* (Glasgow, 1999), p. 149. See also the entry for Charlotte Anne Waldie in the *Oxford DNB*.
67 McMillan, *The Scotswoman at Home and Abroad*, p. 144
68 P.H. Scott, "The last Purely Scotch Age' in D. Gifford, (ed.), *The History of Scottish Literature, Volume Three: The Nineteenth Century* (Aberdeen, 1988), p. 18.
69 See the very interesting article by G. Morton. 'What if?: The Significance of Scotland's Missing Nationalism in the Nineteenth Century' in Broun, Finlay and Lynch, *Image and Identity*, pp. 157-176.
70 Edinburgh Central Library, *Copy of the Petition presented to HER MAJESTY THE QUEEN From her Scottish Subjects, Protesting against the Official Misuse of the National Names, in Violation of the Provisions of the Treaty Of Union between Scotland and England of 1707; with Statement and Appendix thereto* (Edinburgh, 1897).

71 Edinburgh Central Library, *Copy of the Petition*, II. EXTRACTS FROM THE QUEEN'S SPEECHES TO PARLIAMENT.
72 Edinburgh Central Library, *Copy of the Petition*, III. TREATIES AND OTHER AGREEMENTS WITH FOREIGN POWERS. Agreement between Great Britain and Turkey, dated Constantinople, 14 August 1878
73 Edinburgh Central Library, *Copy of the Petition*, VIII. INSCRIPTION ON MONUMENT AT INKERMANN, "ERECTED BY THE BRITISH ARMY".
74 Murdoch, *Network North*, p. 65. For more on Durie's mission see ibid, pp. 280-312.

'UNION IS NOT AMALGAMATION. SCOTLAND IS A NATION': UNIONISM AND SCOTTISHNESS IN THE TWENTIETH CENTURY

Paul Ward

Abstract

The Conservatives, known as Unionists, were a popular force in Scotland for much of the twentieth century because they were well able to represent Scottish interests and identity within the British political system. Their decline, which came later than many historians suggest, accompanied a move away from Unionism towards Conservatism. This was epitomised by the disregard for Scotland exhibited by Thatcherism. However, Labour's ability to express Scottishness in the 1980s and 1990s meant that the decline of Conservatism in Scotland should not be seen as the demise of unionism.

Three hundred years on, the Union is unlikely to result in enthusiastic celebrations of its longevity.[1] The opening of the Scottish Parliament in 1999 was lauded as the return of governance to Scotland for the first time in three centuries, as if it ended subordination by an imperial authority. It was widely seen as a new departure, transforming the historic direction of Scotland. Such transformational moments often have the effect of downplaying parts of the past that do not complement the present. Scotland's move towards autonomy, however limited, is likely to see commentators lessening the historical significance of those who opposed devolution. Alex Salmond, leader of the Scottish National Party in 1999, told the assembled Members of the Scottish Parliament that 'Today, even as we celebrate, we remember people of all political parties who devoted themselves to achieving self-government for Scotland, but who never lived to see this day.'[2] The implication is that those who devoted themselves to the Union will not be remembered as well as its opponents will be. Yet, the existence of the Union for three hundred years and probably for some substantial time to come demands explanation.

It can be boldly stated that the Union survived because it was well supported in Scotland for much of those three centuries. This essay examines the experience of Scottish Unionism in the twentieth century as a political and cultural force that was able to regenerate constantly because the Union delivered so much of what so many of the Scottish people desired. The essay does so by differentiating varieties of Unionism. First, much of the essay examines the Unionism of the Conservative Party in Scotland. The Conservatives enjoyed a remarkably long period of political dominance in Scotland, particularly in the 1930s and 1950s and the forces contributing to this political support will be discussed. Secondly, this essay will briefly examine the relationship of the Liberal and Labour parties to unionism and national identity, arguing that however insensitive or even hostile to political nationalism these forces sometimes were, their unionism could accommodate Scottish national identity. The essay concludes with some speculative comments suggesting that unionism remains powerful in post-devolution Scotland because of its remarkable flexibility.

Unionism and 'British' History

The incontrovertible decline of the Conservatives in Scotland in the late twentieth century has encouraged many anti-Conservative historians and political activists to see the party's earlier success as aberrant and temporary. This is closely linked to the hypothesis that Britishness was but a temporary identity whose moment would not last.[3] There is an inference that study of such momentary ideas is not necessarily the most useful task for historians, who might switch their concern to histories of those people who are currently fulfilling their historic duty of nation-building rather than those, like the British, who have turned out to be 'non-historic'. There has rightly been a historiographical renaissance in Scotland and Wales alongside political devolution since 1997.[4] Yet one aspect of this new academic study seeks to divorce Scotland and Wales from their British pasts. Hence, in Welsh Studies John Osmond has recently argued that Britain 'no longer provides the essential lens through which Wales and what it means to be Welsh has to be viewed [...]. Welsh identity is no longer to be nationalized within Britain.'[5] This essay welcomes the increasing importance of Scottish and Welsh historiography, because it offers a much-needed antidote to the Anglo-centric version of history that for so long held sway in 'British history'. However, 'British' history remains vital because Scotland, Wales and England were and remain part of a wider political and cultural nation. As Richard Finlay has argued: 'What is needed [...] is British history from a Scottish perspective.'[6]

The Conservative Party in Scotland is one example of where this approach may usefully be applied. The party cannot be understood outside the mindset in which supporters of the party operated. As James Kellas has argued, 'It has always been the party of British nationalism: of the Union and the Empire.'[7] The collapse of the party's support in the last decades of the twentieth century has encouraged some commentators to connect the decline of the Conservatives with the decline of Britishness and unionism, seeing them as parallel. The failure of the Conservatives to win a single seat in the 1997 general election allowed some to crow that not only the Unionists but the Union had met its inevitable demise. Of course it is necessary to disentangle support for *a* unionist party from support for the Union, but it is also imperative not to throw the baby out with the bathwater in declarations of Tory weakness in Scotland and Scottishness. Conservatives in Scotland were unashamedly Unionist – indeed between 1912 and 1965 the party was officially called the Unionist Party. The party was later to face many accusations of Englishness and indeed recognised this as a problem itself. In the late 1960s, the party's research centre warned that the Conservatives had 'got an exceedingly bad image. It is thought to be out of touch, a bastion of "foreign" (English) privilege, Westminster-orientated, associated with recalcitrant landowners.'[8]

The Unionists and Scotland: Ascendancy
For most of the twentieth century the party may have been 'British' but it was also undoubtedly Scottish. What the Checklands point out about the nineteenth century, that 'It was a curious circumstance that the Conservatives did more to recognize Scottish claims than the Liberal Party so favoured by the Scots,' also applies to much of the twentieth century.[9] In the nineteenth century Scottishness was mostly associated with Liberalism, which was able to make substantial electoral in-roads in Scotland. However, Scottishness did not mean nationalism and the issue of Irish Home Rule led substantial numbers of Scottish Liberals to abandon Gladstone's pluralist vision of the Union and to go over, eventually, to the Conservative Party, transforming it into the Unionist Party. The Conservatives further benefited from association with Protestantism in contrast to the Catholicism of many immigrants attracted by employment opportunities in Scotland. These new supporters did not doubt the Conservatives' attachment to Scotland. Already the Conservatives under Lord Salisbury had established the office of the Secretary of Scotland in 1885 and in 1926 Stanley Baldwin, the most English of British Prime Ministers, raised the status of this post to that of Secretary of State. The weakness of the Conservatives in the era of Tariff Reform was largely overcome after 1918 and British government saw a substantial Scottish contribution. Hence, in varying ways Scots like Lord Weir, Sir James Lithgow, Lords Maclay and Inverforth, Sir Eric and Sir Auckland Geddes and Andrew Bonar Law made politics truly British (and between 1916 and 1922 the United Kingdom had a Welsh Prime Minister in Lloyd George).

John Foster has said of this group that, 'They were not [in London] specifically as Scots, certainly not as any form of lobby. They were present as British business leaders and politicians to chart the way forward for the world's biggest (and recently victorious) imperial power.'[10] The Union was seen as providing possibilities for Scottish partnership rather than absorption.

This was the beginning rather than the end of the Scottish contribution to British Conservative politics.[11] There was a sense of Scottish personality in British Conservatism between the wars. Some prominent Scots such as Bob Boothby and Katherine, Duchess of Atholl, could be described as mavericks but their contribution was no less significant for that.[12] Noel Skelton, MP for the Scottish Universities, coined the phrase of 'the property-owning democracy' that would play so much part in twentieth-century Conservatism. John Buchan, another Universities MP, emphasised his Scottishness in politics and culture, easily expressing the multi-national and imperial nature of the British imperial ruling elite from his home in Oxfordshire and, after 1935, from his residence in Ottawa as Governor-General of Canada.

More central was Walter Elliot, who encapsulates the relationship between Scottishness and the Union in Conservative politics in the mid-twentieth century. A discussion of Elliot's career shows how 'Scotland did not cease to be a nation or a civil society in 1707 [...]. Instead, Scots took the full opportunities which England and the empire provided, and were in no way confined to the subaltern tasks.'[13] Elliot maintained an extremely close connection to Scotland even while seeking the highest political offices within the UK. After traditional apprenticeship as parliamentary under-secretary in the 1920s he became, in succession, Financial Secretary to the Treasury, Minister of Agriculture, Secretary of State for Scotland and Minister of Health. At no point did involvement in British politics mean turning his back on Scotland, to which he was connected through birth, education, ownership of land, and as a constituency MP.

Being Scottish was fundamental to Elliot's personal and political identities. In his major contribution to Conservative thought in the 1920s, *Toryism and the Twentieth Century*, he concluded that 'History shows the extraordinary strength and persistence of national characteristics, and the success of policy based upon these.'[14] Elliot marked Scotland out as distinct from England; indeed he foregrounded historical conflict between the two nations. During the Second World War he described the counties of northern England through which he had travelled: 'Over by Lancaster and Preston, down to Carlisle and the country of the Border wars. Talk about scorched earth – Scotland had nothing to learn in those old days. "They crossed Liddel at curfew hour

– And burned my little lonely tower."' These wars, Elliot argued, had 'kept Scotland independent'.[15] Such emphasis contributed to the Scottish sense of the Union as a partnership of equals, or as Graeme Morton has usefully characterised it, Unionist-nationalism.[16]

The survival of separate Scottish legal, educational and religious institutions after the Union allowed many Scots to see themselves as a nation even though they lacked a state. Elliot was appointed Lord High Commissioner to the General Assembly of the Church of Scotland in 1956, representing the crown to the established church in Scotland, emphasising the potential for diversity of structures, traditions and history within the Union. Elliot described the Church of Scotland as 'the characteristic gathering' of 'the political heritage of Scotland.'[17]

This support for institutions linked Scots further into the UK through the contribution of Scottish regiments to the British Army. Whereas Scottish education, law and religion operated in parallel with the institutions of the rest of the UK, the army well represents what Keith Robbins has described as 'the blending of "the English", "the Scots", and "the Welsh" to produce "the British".'[18] Like so many Scots, Elliot's service in the army during both world wars encouraged consideration of the similarities between Britons as well as the differences between the nations within the UK. The Scottish regiments became an essential, and undoubtedly conservative, component in the construction of Scottishness within the Union.

The outbreak of the Second World War enabled an attempt at restoration of Scottish confidence after the crisis of the 1930s, caused by economic weakness, mass unemployment and its accompanying social problems.[19] Again, Scotland had the opportunity to add its industry and manpower to a worthwhile international cause. In this instance, though, the experience of Elliot and other Scottish Unionists diverged from that of the wider nation. Elliot served again in the army but his military service in the Second World War is associated with his political failure to oppose appeasement in the 1930s.[20] Support for Neville Chamberlain's policy was strong in Scottish Unionism; hence when Winston Churchill became Prime Minister in 1940, Elliot found himself outside the government and the Scottish influence in British Conservatism was substantially weakened.[21]

Yet the Second World War re-established the essential importance of an industrial economy and once more raised the significance of Scotland. This contribution to the British global role was a continuation of Scotland's major role in the development of the empire.[22] Unlike many of his Scottish contemporaries, Elliot had no direct role or material interest in the Empire yet he enjoyed a strong sentimental attachment to it and as Scottish Secretary was instrumental in organising the Glasgow Empire Exhibition of 1938 as an attempt to revive the Scottish economy. At the same time, the transfer of many of the functions of the Scottish Office from London to Edinburgh suggested Unionist sensitivities. Other Unionists were equally clear that the Empire had a substantial part to play in Scottish development.[23] The Second World War, while often considered in its domestic context, was also an imperial war, and Unionists contributed as imperialists as well as Scots.

Domestic issues were, however, most important in the general election of 1945, which saw the landslide victory of Labour. In Scotland, though, the Unionists fared better than elsewhere in the UK. While the number of Unionist MPs fell from 45 to 30, their share of the vote fell only from 42 to 40.3 per cent, compared with a fall from 47.7 to 39.8 per cent across the UK. In a period when Labour were secure in government, Elliot developed a distinctive political idea that placed the Conservatives exactly where they wished to be in terms of their relationship to Scotland. Defeated in the 1945 election, Elliot fought and won the Scottish Universities by-election in 1946. In his address, he rallied to the defence of Scotland in the face of what he said was centralising Labour legislation:

> The legislative Union between Scotland and England was never meant to entail, and should not entail, a complete swamping of the economic identity of the Northern Kingdom such as is now being conducted in the name of nationalisation. The transfer by statute of the control of the whole of Scottish industry to Westminster is not nationalisation, it is de-nationalisation.[24]

In the late 1940s, Scottish Unionism recaptured its vitality even while British Conservatism struggled to come to terms with Labour's victory and programme. Within the party a committee was established to consider Scotland's relationship to government and, based on Elliot's arguments, it was concluded that:

> Unionism is not amalgamation. Scotland is a nation [...]. It is only since 1945, under the first socialist majority, that we have seen the policy of amalgamation superseding that of Union. This must inevitably result from the fulfilment of the socialist creed, which is basically one of amalgamation and centralisation. To this policy we are fundamentally opposed.[25]

In the late 1940s and early 1950s there was a flurry of nationalist activity around the National Covenant, which collected two million signatures in support of Home Rule.[26] Yet such popular activities did not transform into electoral support for nationalism, much to the dismay of the SNP, who gathered less than 10,000 votes in the 1950 and 1951 elections. Instead these were the peak years of Unionist ascendancy. The Conservatives share of the Scottish vote rose at the expense of the Liberals, who saw their support fall below two per cent in 1955. This reflects the Unionist success in appealing to an anti-socialist vote as well as its ability to appeal to the persistent desire for devolution among many Liberals. In the 1950s Conservative governments at Westminster further strengthened the Scottish Office by adding a Minister of State who would reside mainly in Edinburgh, established a Royal Commission on Scottish Affairs and passed more functions over to the Scottish Office.

The culmination of the Unionists' ability to represent Scottishness, at the same time as a world economic boom moderated the weakness of Scotland's declining industrial economy, came when the party achieved 50.1 per cent of the Scottish vote in 1955. Most observers comment only on this election as the moment before the fall, skirting over the tremendous achievement entailed in securing a majority of the popular vote in Scotland. Foster has remarked that despite low unemployment, improved health and housing, and lowered infant mortality, 'Scottish historians have tended to see the stability of the 1950s as an end rather than a beginning.' Agreeing with this view, he argues that the situation was 'inherently unstable'.[27] A reduction in the Unionist share of the vote was inevitable after 1955 and the fact that in 1959 it fell by less than three percent (though compared to a fall of under half a per cent across the UK) means that seeing the 1950s as both the apotheosis and the beginning of the end can only be justified by hindsight and some wishful thinking. A more substantial decrease occurred between 1959 and 1964, when the Unionist share of vote in Scotland fell by 6.6 per cent, but this almost matched the 'British' experience because the Conservatives lost 6 per cent across the UK.

The tail-end of the Conservatives' thirteen years in power does not suggest substantial divergence of experience within the Union in this period, though undoubtedly a distinctive Scottish element was apparent in some aspects of the swing of the pendulum against the government. One part of Labour's assault on the Tories was that they were out of date, contributing to the stagnant society through their protection of the vested interests of the Establishment. The succession of Sir Alec Douglas-Home to the premiership aided Labour's assault and Scottish Unionists failed to rebut the accusations of being behind the times. Lady Tweedsmuir, Under-Secretary at the Scottish Office between 1962 and 1964, claimed that 'Modernisation [is] not a catchphrase but a fact. The power stations, nuclear and conventional, the new factories and industries [...] and the miles of new roads, are transforming the face of Scotland.' Such achievements were not enough to save her seat in

Aberdeen or those of six other Scottish Unionists.[28] It might be said that for once, having a Scottish leader of the British party damaged the party in Scotland, but this was not out of sorts with the experience in the rest of Britain. It was remarkably easy in Scotland to see Home as epitomizing all that was worst about upper-class anglicized Scots.

The Long Decline

With the loss of seven seats in Scotland, the party spent the rest of the 1960s scrabbling around for policies to avert continued decline. They sought to address the allegation of out-datedness. With Edward Heath as the new Conservative leader, the party decided the label of Unionism was holding them back. In an attempt to capture a sense of youthfulness, the party in Scotland was reorganized and its name changed. Unionism was seen as being of less significance to the electorate in a period of concern about the Scottish industrial economy. The Conservatives had decided to continue to take on Harold Wilson in the language of modernization that he had chosen. In 1964 and 1966 the Conservatives were concerned about Labour's ability to improve their vote and number of seats in Scotland. In 1964 Labour won five additional seats and in 1966 three more. Whereas in the 1950s the parties had an almost equal number of seats, by the mid-1960s the number of Labour MPs was more than double that of the Conservatives. The Conservatives' concern focused on the continuing loss of the Protestant working-class vote as a result of secularization and the decline of sectarianism.[29]

The SNP, on the other hand, mustered only 5 per cent of the vote in 1966. The Conservatives removed Unionism from their name because they did not see political nationalism as an issue. The interesting point here is that it suggests that the rise of the SNP was not, at the time, perceived as gradual and inexorable. When it came, it came rapidly, and, it is fair to say, over the next thirty years the Conservatives mishandled the defence of the Union to their electoral cost in both Scotland and Wales. For a start, the Conservatives, like Labour, exaggerated the strength of nationalism. The SNP won the Hamilton by-election in November 1966. Despite the fact that it was a safe Labour seat in an area where the Conservatives had never done well, Heath declared Scottish nationalism 'the biggest single factor in our politics today'.[30] There was, within the Conservatives' history, substantial potential to respond to the demands for the expression of Scottish nationality, yet Heath's response in the 'Declaration of Perth' at the Scottish party conference in 1968 did not seem to grow out of the Scottish party but instead gave the impression of English interference. The so-called Thistle Group, launched in 1967, and other Scottish Conservatives had already recommended a partly elected assembly. At Perth, Heath announced that he was forming the grandly named Constitutional Committee, chaired by Home, which he had instructed to recommend an assembly. The effect was to make it appear that Scottish policy-making emerged from the English (and the anglicised Scot) and from expedience rather than principle.

Heath's posturing did not restore the electoral fortunes of the party in Scotland, though it did temporarily slow the decline. The party won the 1970 general election and three additional seats in Scotland though its vote there rose by less than half of one per cent. However, the SNP, though it achieved a respectable share of the vote, did not make its predicted breakthrough. The Conservatives in office considered that they had more pressing 'British' problems to deal with and implemented none of the Home committee's recommendations. The economic crisis had dramatic effects on the electoral fortunes of the Conservatives, exacerbated north of the border by the particularly severe problems of manufacturing industry. This was expressed in the workers' occupation of the Upper Clyde Shipyards in 1971 and 1972, which forced the Conservative government to back down on its claims that it would allow market forces to regulate the economy.[31] The SNP were unable to mount a challenge on the economics of crisis until the discovery of oil in the North Sea but they only further dented the damaged British Conservatives rather than being responsible for their decline. Between 1970 and the second election of 1974 the number of Scots prepared to vote Conservative fell from just about four in ten to less than a quarter (24.7 per cent). While the situation in Scotland was severe, it did still mirror, in exaggerated form, what was happening elsewhere in the UK. The Tories' share of the vote fell by 13 per cent in Scotland and by just over 10 per cent elsewhere.

Pretty much whatever policy the Conservatives came up with for Scotland was unlikely to prevent their decline. There was nothing distinctive, for example, about the Conservatives' claim to be a devolution party.[32] With the fall of Heath and the election of Margaret Thatcher to the leadership, the party had reached a turning point that would prove to be of fundamental importance to the fortunes of the party, and indeed for the shape of the Union.

The Conservatives had the advantage of being in opposition while the Labour government, insincerely and unconvincingly, attempted to charter devolution bills for Scotland and Wales through Parliament. Thatcher considered herself 'an instinctive Unionist'.[33] She wavered in the 1970s, supporting the creation of a directly-elected assembly at the Scottish party conference in 1976,[34] yet Thatcher saw the devolution episode as evidence of a wider crisis which had affected the status of Britain in the eyes of the world. Britain was by now a member of the European Economic Community, was fighting an undeclared war in Northern Ireland, and experienced the wave of strikes in 1979 known as the 'winter of discontent'.[35] In such circumstances, Thatcher's promise to end the crisis and make Britain great again had much resonance, especially in England but also in Scotland and Wales. The devolution referendums turned into something of a fiasco. In Wales only one in five of those who voted supported devolution. In Scotland, a majority of those who voted did support self-government, yet the amendment to the Scotland Act which required 40 per cent of the entire Scottish electorate to vote 'yes' put paid to a renegotiation of the Union. On 28 March 1979 the SNP MPs punished those they held responsible for the debacle, supporting a Conservative motion of no confidence in the Labour government. In the resulting election, the Conservatives did well across the UK. Their vote rose in Scotland by 6.7 per cent, while that of the SNP fell by 13.1 per cent.

Thatcherism and Scotland: Tory Rout

Thatcher offered firm government after years of small or non-existent parliamentary majorities.[36] Thatcher's success, despite mass unemployment in the early 1980s, can be measured by a survey that suggested that 86 per cent of those living in Britain were proud to be British. Richard Rose, the widely respected political scientist at the University of Strathclyde who conducted the survey, argued that 'Because national pride is so widespread in Britain, it is normal in the literal sense, that is, it is the norm to which nearly everyone conforms.'[37] Thatcher believed the lesson of 1979 was that Scotland should be brought into line with the rest of Britain. The paradox was that Thatcher's British patriotic project was to contribute more to the unravelling of the UK than the decade-long crisis of the 1970s. Labour's hold on political loyalty had been under threat in Scotland because of the detrimental effect of economic decline and the availability of protest parties expressing nationalism, yet Labour had never been seriously challenged by the nationalists. Labour's lowest share of the vote between 1945 and 1997 in Scotland was 36 per cent. The nationalists' highest share was 30 per cent. More usually Labour could rely on more than 40 per cent in Scotland, whereas the nationalists' share after 1970 averaged only 18.8 per cent. Mainly this was because Labour had delivered on the promise of a welfare state after the Second World War. The socialisation of the state had been accomplished within a language of British nationalism. Its institutions were 'national' and 'British': the National Health Service, British Railways and National Insurance. The Scottish contribution to Labour had been extensive from the party's foundation and Scottish (and Welsh) socialists had ensured that the welfare state was *British* rather than *English*. Thatcher believed that dependence on the welfare state was a fundamental source of Britain's weakness. Her desire to 'roll back the frontiers of the state' was particularly hard felt in Scotland for, as her memoirs record, 'public expenditure per head in Scotland was far higher than in England' and hence, 'the conditions of dependency were strongly present.'[38] In undermining 'dependency' Thatcher undermined her party in Scotland. She made absolute the divorce between Unionism and Scottishness and by 1997 no Conservatives were returned to Westminster from Scotland.

The inability of Scottish voters to shape government policy led to the renewed growth of nationalism. By the end of the 1980s, one in five voters in Scotland supported the SNP. There was a widespread feeling that 'British' politics lacked legitimacy. In particular, the introduction of the Community Charge (known as the poll tax) to finance local authorities in Scotland, a year before England and Wales, suggested that Scotland could not even rely on equality of treatment within the Union, despite Thatcher's earlier claims.

Other Unionists

If the Union had to rely upon the Conservatives alone then its survival would have been much more in doubt at the end of the century. However, other 'British' parties, committed to the Union, were also able to represent Scottish distinctiveness and to better adjust to the emerging Scottish desire for self-government. In the 1970s Labour's turn to devolution had looked cynical and self-serving, caused by its weak electoral position and reliance on Scottish and Welsh voters. There were determined opponents within the Scottish and Welsh parties, and it was a Scottish Labour MP, George Cunningham, who sat for Islington, who had introduced the amendment requiring forty per cent of the Scottish electorate to vote yes in the 1979 referendum before devolution legislation would be introduced. Yet Labour's share of the vote rose by 5 per cent between 1974 and 1979, to 41.5 per cent. Much of the Scottish electorate still considered the party best able to represent Scottish interests.

In the Thatcher years, Labour underwent an 'intellectual reorientation' in its attitudes towards devolution.[39] Many of the British party leaders such as John Smith, Donald Dewar and Gordon Brown were sincere proponents of devolution and the party participated fully in the Scottish Constitutional Convention launched in 1989 contributing to the recommendation that a parliament with wide legislative powers be formed in Edinburgh. Labour benefited from nationalism in the 1980s and 1990s rather than being damaged by it. This was not just a return to the 1970s for Scottish Labour but the revival of a longer tradition of pluralist Britishness within British politics of the left going back to the late nineteenth century. The recognition of national distinctiveness was seen as a policy for strengthening the Union of the UK, which was widely seen as a progressive force on the left. Hence Gladstone considered that 'the true supporters of the union are those who firmly uphold the supreme authority of parliament, but exercise that authority to bind the three nations by the indissoluble tie of liberal and equal laws.'[40] While responding to the nationalist challenge in Ireland, the British Left came to see the solution in a plural rather than monolithic approach to the political representation of national identities in the UK.

The *British* parties were responding to challenges from the 'periphery' but often those challenges came from within their parties. Home Rule Bills were introduced for Scotland and Wales before the First World War by Liberals and in the inter-war years and after 1945 by Labour MPs. Neither the Liberals nor Labour were English parties. Both drew considerable strength from Scotland and Wales. In the mid-century Labour abandoned much of its interest in political pluralism. Unemployment and industrial weakness came to be seen as problems that could only be solved by all-British planning. Tom Johnston, later Secretary of State for Scotland, explained his rejection of the 'form of Scots nationalism which had lost itself in Jacobite mists [...] all London Scots Labourmen [were] vastly more disturbed that Scotland's unemployment relative to her population was 68½% worse than England's [...] that our maternal mortality was 50% higher than it was south of the border.' The solution, however, 'lay not in heraldic restoration but in social ownership of soil, industry, and finance, and there was one political route and one only to social ownership: it was through the British Labour Party.'[41] By the 1950s the Labour Party, having experienced majority government that enabled the establishment of the social democratic welfare state, felt little need to consider political devolution to Scotland. Despite this, the party's electoral performance in Scotland remained strong in every election except those in 1974 and 1983. In the late 1960s and 1970s Labour's interest in devolution was only aroused by the sense of electoral threat but the ability to respond to calls for constitutional change was created by the nature of Labour as a 'multi-national coalition party' that secured support in all parts of Britain.[42]

Labour was able to maintain this performance despite insensitivity to the demands of political nationalists because such demands were few and infrequent for much of the twentieth century and, when they came, Labour was able to accommodate them within its overall sense of pluralism. It was able to do so more convincingly than the Liberals, who had retained a much more consistent commitment to devolution. Jo Grimond, Liberal leader between 1956 and 1967, wrote in his autobiography that a 'suggestion Liberals pursued in and out of season was home rule for Scotland and Wales. In every Election address I issued I proclaimed it.'[43] Three main factors prevented the Liberals from seriously challenging Labour. Being a minority party meant that the Liberals could not deliver social reform as Labour could do. As T.C. Smout argues, 'the power of the Labour party in Scotland rested unequivocally on two distinctively Scottish class facts – living in a council house and the threat of unemployment.'[44] But neither were the Liberals as clear on devolution as appearances suggest, for in the 1970s, Grimond, briefly party leader in 1976, was equivocal on the Scotland Bill. 'I never guessed,' he wrote, 'that [devolution] would take the form of an additional tier loaded on to a country bent double under too much government.'[45] Finally, the Liberals' major contest for votes was with the SNP. Whereas in Britain as a whole in the 1970s, the Liberals' claim to be the third party was strong, in Scotland the SNP vote passed that of the Liberals in 1970 and remained higher until 1983. In such circumstances, Labour was able to establish itself as the party of Scotland in the late 1980s and early 1990s.

The End of Empire
The 'British' political parties have acted as essential props of the Union. Other than the nationalists, all political parties in the UK have been unionist. Together, they have secured the support of the substantial majority of voters in Britain.[46] They have meant that while other props of the Union have been removed, the Union has not collapsed. The chief of these props has often been seen as the Empire, which was certainly fundamental in the expression of Scottishness from the eighteenth to the twentieth centuries. The end of Empire in the late twentieth century has been seen by many as undermining the Union. Angus Calder has argued that 'And came, as the disintegration of Empire deprived Scots of the basis of their British identity, the first real electoral impact – ever – of Scottish Nationalism, in the late 1960s'.[47] Other historians have questioned the linkage, in part because the end of Empire, and particularly the growing autonomy of the white Dominions with which Scotland was most associated, and the (limited) rise of nationalism do not

coincide.⁴⁸ T.M. Devine has convincingly argued that as the Empire came to be seen as less economically important to Scotland in the period of industrial decline so it came to be seen as less culturally important.⁴⁹ Both Conservative and Labour parties addressed economic weakness through the rhetoric of the welfare state, modernisation and later through the turn to European integration. On the one hand, as Finlay argues, 'The era of the Welfare State and the managed economy revitalised the Union and made material sense to the Scots.'⁵⁰ On the other, some Unionists, however imperially minded, could see Scotland's links to Europe providing the potential for revitalisation. At the Foreign Office in the 1970s, Lady Tweedsmuir, daughter-in-law of John Buchan, explained how:

> Without undue pride I can say that Scots have skills and ideas to contribute to the growth of Europe and we still have the Scottish qualities of perseverance, spiced with ambition, which helped to forge the prototype of all Common Markets – the Union of Scotland and England two and a half centuries ago.⁵¹

The passing of the Empire did not, therefore, lead to the end of the Union.

Conclusion

Without doubt, the popularity of the Union and allegiance to Britishness has experienced a decline in the late twentieth century. However, Conservative dominance in Scotland from the 1920s to the late 1950s cannot be dismissed as a mere moment. While the Conservatives associated themselves with Scottishness within Unionism they did remarkably well. Only when they began to see Unionism as out-dated and turned to a language of Conservatism associated with modernity did their decline become more serious. When they took up a programme of devolution in the late 1960s it seemed a product of desperation rather than principle. Even so, Conservative decline did not mean the end of the Union, for Labour was able to rediscover devolution in the 1980s. Thatcher's attacks on the welfare state helped to encourage the growth of demands for political devolution which can be seen as an attempt to defend the implicit Britishness of Labour's 1940s programme.

In a fit of optimism, Tom Nairn declared in 2001 that 'A dissolution of the old multi-national state is indeed under way, and there is now almost no one who believes otherwise.'⁵² The Union was at an end and Scotland had returned. In January 2007, on the tercentenary of the Union, a poll by the BBC, itself an institution encouraging continuing Britishness, suggested otherwise. The BBC asked 543 people in Scotland, 'Would you like the Union to continue as it is or would you like to see it come to an end? If it were to end this would mean that Scotland became an independent country?' The response was surprising enough to be newsworthy for while 174 Scots answered no, 304 or 56 per cent, foresaw a future for the Union. The likelihood is that the majority of those in favour of the Union's continuance saw no incompatibility with their sense of Scottishness. That was the genius of the Union.

Notes

1. Indeed, the commemoration is taking the form of debates, showing the ambiguities of marking a event that has become contested in the present. Examples include, BBC *Newsnight*, 16 January 2007 and University of Edinburgh, 'Debating the Union of 1707', 10 January 2007, http://www.ed.ac.uk/news/scotlandunion/debating.html.
2. 'Salmond heralds new chapter', http://news.bbc.co.uk/1/hi/special_report/1999/ 06/99/scottish_parliament_opening/382683.stm Accessed December 2007.
3. Christopher Harvie, 'The Moment of British Nationalism, 1939-1970,' *Political Quarterly*, 71 (2000), pp. 328-40.
4. For example, R.A. Houston and W.W.J. Knox (eds), *The New Penguin History of Scotland From the Earliest Times to the Present Day* (London: Penguin/National Museums of Scotland, 2002), Murray G.H. Pittock, *A New History of Scotland* (Stroud: Sutton, 2003), Richard J. Finlay, 'New Britain, New Scotland, New History? The Impact of Devolution on the Development of Scottish Historiography', *Journal of Contemporary History*, 36, 2 (2001), pp. 383-93.
5. John Osmond, 'Welsh politics in the new Millennium', in David Morley and Kevin Robins, eds., *British Cultural Studies* (Oxford: Oxford University Press, 2001), pp. 109-10. I owe this reference to Martin Johnes.
6. Richard J. Finlay, 'Scotland in the Twentieth Century: In Defence of Oligarchy?' *Scottish Historical Review*, 73 (1994), p. 105. See also his *A Partnership for Good? Scottish Politics and the Union since 1880* (Edinburgh: John Donald, 1997).
7. James Kellas, 'The Party in Scotland', in Anthony Seldon and Stuart Ball (eds), *Conservative Century: The Conservative Party since 1900* (Oxford: Oxford University Press, 1994), p. 690.
8. John Ramsden, *The Winds of Change: Macmillan to Heath 1957-1975* (Harlow: Longman, 1996), pp. 405-6.
9. Sydney and Olive Checkland, *Industry and Ethos: Scotland 1832-1914* (London: Edward Arnold, 1984), p. 170.
10. John Foster, 'The Twentieth Century, 1914-1979' in Houston and Knox (eds), *The New Penguin History of Scotland*, pp. 427-8.
11. See in particular, I.G.C. Hutchison, *Scottish Politics in the Twentieth Century* (Basingstoke: Palgrave, 2001).
12. Kellas, 1994, pp. 685-8.
13. David McCrone, 'Unmasking Britannia: The Rise and Fall of British National Identity,'

Nations and Nationalism, 3 (1997), p. 584.
[14] Walter Elliot, *Toryism and the Twentieth Century* (London: Philip Allen, 1927), p. 4.
[15] Walter Elliot, 'Calling Australia: A Journey in War-Time', 19 March 1942, Walter Elliot Papers, Acc. 6721/1/3, National Library of Scotland (NLS). Elliot is quoting Sir Walter Scott, 'The Lay of the Last Minstrel', c.1802.
[16] Graeme Morton, *Unionist-Nationalism: Governing Urban Scotland, 1830-1860* (East Linton: Tuckwell, 1999).
[17] Walter Elliot, 'Scottish Politics', in the Duke of Atholl (ed.), *A Scotsman's Heritage* (London: Alexander Maclehose, 1932), pp. 58-9.
[18] Keith Robbins, *Nineteenth-Century Britain: England, Scotland, and Wales The Making of a Nation* (Oxford: Oxford University Press, 1988), p. 2.
[19] Richard J. Finlay, 'National Identity in Crisis: Politicians, Intellectuals and the "End of Scotland"', *History*, 79 (1994), pp. 242-59.
[20] See Paul Ward, *Unionism in the United Kingdom, 1918-1974* (Basingstoke: Palgrave Macmillan, 2005), pp. 28-30.
[21] Foster, 2002, p. 453.
[22] The major work is Michael Fry's *The Scottish Empire* (Edinburgh: Tuckwell and Birlinn, 2001).
[23] For the Empire's domestic impact see John M. MacKenzie, 'Empire and National Identities: The Case of Scotland', *Transactions of the Royal Historical Society*, 6th series, 8, 1998, pp. 215-31.
[24] Elliot Papers, Acc. 6721/1/1, NLS.
[25] Conservative Party, 'Scottish Control of Scottish Affairs', 1949, quoted in Ward, p. 33.
[26] Finlay, 1997, pp. 140-42.
[27] Foster, 2002, p. 464.
[28] General Election Campaign, September-October 1964, Speeches, Lady Tweedsmuir Papers, Acc. 11884/21, NLS.
[29] James Mitchell, *Conservatives and the Union: A Study of Conservative Party Attitudes to Scotland* (Edinburgh: Edinburgh University Press, 1990), pp. 10-11.
[30] Richard Crossman recorded Heath making this comment. Quoted in Mitchell, 1990, p. 55.
[31] Foster, 2002, p. 476.
[32] See for example Scottish Conservative and Unionist Central Office, *Freedom for all the People: A Charter for Scotland* Edinburgh, September 1974
[33] Vernon Bogdanor, *Devolution in the United Kingdom* (Oxford: Oxford University Press, 2001) p. 137.
[34] Vernon Bogdanor, 'Devolution', Zig Layton-Henry (ed.), *Conservative Party Politics* (Basingstoke: Macmillan, 1981) pp. 75-94 offers a concise account of the Conservatives and devolution.
[35] See Phillip Whitehead, *The Writing on the Wall: Britain in the 1970s* (London: Michael Joseph, 1985) for the perspective of devolution as part of a wider 'British' crisis.
[36] Some parts of what follows have previously been published in Paul Ward,

'Devolution and Britishness, 1966-1999,' in C. Civardi and M. Jones (eds), *Revue Française de Civilisation Britannique: La Dévolution des Pouvoirs à L'Ecosse et Au Pays Galles, 1966-1999* (Paris: Centre de Recherches et d'Etude en Civilisation Britannique, 2006).

37 Quoted in Paul Ward, *Britishness since 1870* (London: Routledge, 2004), p. 8.
38 Margaret Thatcher, *The Downing Street Years* (New York: HarperCollins, 1993), pp. 620, 619.
39 Hutchison, 2001, pp. 149, 130.
40 Eugenio Biagini, *Gladstone* (Basingstoke: Palgrave, 2000) p. 97.
41 'Scottish Home Rule and Administrative Devolution', Thomas Johnston Papers, Acc. 5862/8, National Library of Scotland.
42 Eugenio Biagini (ed.), *Citizenship and Community: Liberals, Radicals and Collective Identities in the British Isles, 1865-1931* (Cambridge: Cambridge University Press, 1996), p. 2.
43 Jo Grimond, *Memoirs* (London: Heinemann, 1979), p. 208-9.
44 T.C. Smout, 'Scotland 1850-1950', in Thompson, F.M.L. (ed.), *The Cambridge Social History of Britain 1750-1950 Volume I: Regions and Communities* (Cambridge: Cambridge University Press, 1990), p. 242.
45 Grimond, 1979, p. 209.
46 Northern Ireland, outside Britain, is the exception here. See Ward, 2005, chapters 8-10.
47 Angus Calder, *Revolving Culture: Notes from the Scottish Republic* (London: IB Tauris, 1994), p. 9.
48 Hutchison, 2001, pp. 121-2.
49 T.M. Devine, 'The Break-up of Britain? Scotland and the End of Empire', *Transactions of the Royal Historical Society*, no. 16 (2006), pp. 163-80.
50 Richard J. Finlay, 'The Rise and Fall of Popular Imperialism in Scotland 1850-1950', *Scottish Geographical Magazine*, 113 (1997), p. 20.
51 'Speech at dinner for Vice-President of the Commission of the European Communities', 3 February 1972,' Lady Priscilla Tweedsmuir Papers, NLS, Acc. 11884/29.
52 Tom Nairn, *After Britain: New Labour and the Return of Scotland* (London: Granta, 2001), p. 4.

GOVERNING REGIONAL DEVELOPMENT IN PRE-DEVOLUTION SCOTLAND: THATCHERISM AND THE SCOTTISH DEVELOPMENT AGENCY

Henrik Halkier

Abstract

The article explores the relationship between Edinburgh and London in pre-devolution Scotland in order to illuminate the extent to which Scottish political actors could pursue strategies at odds with the views prevailing in British politics. This is done through a case study of the *Scottish Development Agency*, a public body which has been interpreted an example of both the prevalence of London and the resilience of separate Scottish policy agendas. The empirical analysis focus on two critical junctions in the development of the SDA, it is concluded that even in a policy area of great importance for the Thatcher government, the Scottish policy network retained considerable influence on the shaping of regional policy north of the border.

1. Introduction

From the current devolved vantage point, it is easy to portray pre-devolution Scotland as a country ruled from Westminster via the Scottish Office, and writing in the mid-1990s Michael Keating, a leading expert on Scottish politics, argued that 'the real power of decision making lies in the Cabinet and the main Whitehall departments' in London.[1] Other authors have, however, maintained that a distinct 'Scottish political system'[2] or 'semi-state' existed which enjoyed a degree of decision-making autonomy not much different from that of small sovereign nation states like Denmark.[3] While a thorough discussion of the character of pre-devolution governance in Scotland could result in a lengthy and technical text, the aim of this article is more modest, namely to illuminate the relationship between London and Edinburgh in the 1980s by focusing on a case study which would seem to be promising in political terms in that it concerns policy area, regional economic development, where the Conservative Thatcher governments articulated strong liberal views – government subsidies were distorting the market by making firms rely on public handouts – and where a major public body, the *Scottish Development Agency* (SDA), had been established by a Labour government in the 1970s. In short, the case of the SDA during the Thatcher years could serve as a way of probing the political resilience of Edinburgh in circumstances where the London government would clearly seem to have both the motive and the opportunity to bring Scottish public policy into line with the general British approach. Perhaps unsurprisingly, within the existing literature the history of the organisation has been interpreted both as a clear-cut case of London dominance – despite the Agency changing its policies, it was eventually terminated in 1991 as an uncontrollable relic of Labour interventionism[4] – and as an example of successful defence by Edinburgh of Scottish interests because SDA policies were largely unaffected by central government interference throughout the 1980s and beyond.[5]

Drawing on extensive analysis of documentary sources, this text begins by briefly introducing the issues involved in studying Scottish pre-devolution governance and Thatcherism, and then focuses on two critical junctions in the development of the SDA: the change of government in 1979 and its consequences for Agency activities, and the proposal to create a new body, *Scottish Enterprise*, which would comprise the activities hitherto carried out by the Agency.[6] This historical analysis should allow some conclusions to be drawn with regard to the extent to which pre-devolution governance structures were able to guard specific Scottish initiatives in public policy, even under political circumstance that would appear to be less than benevolent.

2. Scotland and Thatcher: Change from Abroad?
In order to understand the conflicts surrounding the SDA in the 1980s, it will be necessary to outline both the political institutions that constituted the framework for pre-devolution governance in Scotland, and the nature of Thatcherism as the agenda-setting political project.

Within the Union State: Pre-Devolution Scottish Governance
When the parliaments of England and Scotland voted for themselves to be replaced by a joint parliament in 1707, they created a unified political superstructure but at the same time explicitly safeguarded the continuation of separate Scottish institutions in central spheres of social life such as law, religion, education and local government, and thus the new 'union state'[7] institutionalised difference within a shared political framework that would allow both countries to enjoy the benefits of a large unified market and access to a growing number of overseas colonies.[8] The setting up in 1885 of the Scottish Office as a decentralised territorial department of central government was designed both to facilitate administrative coordination of public activities and to diffuse political demands for more parliamentary

attention to Scottish matters and for Scottish 'Home Rule',[9] and later the Scottish Office was given responsibility for some, but by no means all, welfare programmes aimed at promoting social and economic development.[10] The Scottish Office was in other words situated at the intersection of two sets of policy networks: the UK-wide functionally defined ones where large London departments like Trade and Industry were the leading actors, and a specific territorial policy network which brought it into frequent contact with Scottish interest organisations and local government,[11] something which had no counterpart 'south of the border' in England. It should, however, also be stressed that while what can be interpreted as a Scottish sub-system operated within the parliament at Westminster with separate parliamentary committees handling Scottish issues,[12] the unitary nature of the British political system was maintained because Scottish legislation was voted on by all MPs and not just those representing Scottish constituencies, and the Scottish Secretary of State and his ministers were appointed by the UK Prime Minister and hence reflect British political views which were not necessarily dominant in Scotland. This distribution of formal political authority made it possible for a government to pursue policies in Scotland which had been rejected at the ballot box by a majority of Scottish voters, but the temptation to do this was of course likely to have been tempered by the importance of the Scottish vote in maintaining the government in power and the extent to which government policies challenged consensual 'Scottish views'.

Given the uniqueness of the Scottish institutional environment compared to other parts of Britain, it is hardly surprising that also political actors and forms of discourse in Scotland have deviated from the British pattern: in addition to issues such as social welfare and economic growth which were high on the agenda all over Britain, Scottish politics was also characterised by the presence of a territorial issue, namely the position of Scotland *vis-à-vis* the rest of the UK, and this manifested itself in two, partly complementary, ways. On the one hand the existence of a Scottish imagined community did not originally result in (or from) the emergence of separatist political movements but rather a pattern of 'dual identities' where varying degrees of identification with Scotland and Britain coexisted also at the level of individual citizens.[13] On the other hand the growth of the Scottish Office clearly encouraged preferential regionalism, i.e. political demands put forward by political actors supporting the union state for special measures to remedy the allegedly unique difficulties facing Scotland.[14] The rise of the Scottish National Party in the late 1960s, pursuing a new territorial politics in the name of 'Scotland-as-nation', did, however, prove to be difficult to counter for Labour and the Conservatives. The dominant parties continued to support the economic and social advantages of the unitary union state, and as the policies proposed by the SNP did not deviate substantially from the existing welfare consensus, the nationalists could still claim that a succession of British governments had failed to address the problems of industrial decline and interregional inequalities effectively. An independent Scotland would, however, have the financial means to pursue such policies much more vigorously on the basis of income generated by the recently discovered North Sea oil,[15] and the extensive use made of the slogan 'It's Scotland's oil'[16] by the SNP in its successful election campaigns for the 1974 general elections suggests that an important part of the party's appeal was the tying together of a separatist nationalist form of territorial politics with the prospects of being able to address longstanding weaknesses of the Scottish economy. It is therefore hardly surprising that in order to counter the rise of political nationalism both Labour and the Conservatives to step up their preferential regionalist efforts to secure positive economic discrimination in favour of Scotland within the union state: both parties suddenly supported a policy proposal they had previously rejected vehemently, namely the setting up of a new semi-autonomous public agency vested with the task of supporting the economic regeneration of the crisis-ridden Scottish economy.[17] As Labour was able to muster a majority in the British parliament after the second general election in 1974, the task of setting up a Scottish Development Agency fell to a government led by Harold Wilson, while the Conservatives replaced Edward Heath with Margaret Thatcher as leader of the parliamentary opposition.

Table 1: Interpreting Thatcherism and the Postwar Consensus
(Source: Halkier, 2006 Table 2.3.)

		Focus	
		Politics	Policy
Change	Extensive	Strategic revolution	Gradual revolution
Change	Limited	Ideational heritage	Implementation failure

Politics of Thatcherism: Interpreting Strategies
The 1979 general election was won by the Conservative party under the leadership of Margaret Thatcher, as were the subsequent elections in 1983 and 1987, and the combination of prime ministerial longevity and a confrontational political style coupled with down-to-earth populist rhetoric probably explains the emergence and durability of 'Thatcherism'.[18] Based

on the assumption that market forces were a superior means of coordinating economic activity, government intervention and trade union influence were seen as inherently distortive and reducing both therefore became goals in their own right. In order to achieve a 'free economy', a 'strong state' was needed, and thus the Conservatives opposed long-term government relationships with vested interests and, indeed, Labour's proposals for devolution in Scotland and Wales.[19] In short, the declared political aims of the new Conservative government were clearly formulated in opposition to the postwar consensus with its welfare-oriented policies which both the major parties had pursued for more than three decades.

The extent to which Thatcherism did indeed constitute a break with the postwar consensus has, however, been widely debated in the academic literature, and as summarised by Table 1 it is possible to identify four basic positions by combining the focus of attention – general politics or implemented policies – with the degree of change identified. The *strategic-revolution* perspective denoted Thatcherism as 'authoritarian populism', a new hegemonic discourse aiming to replace the existing social democratic consensus by a combination of free-market liberalism and organic patriotic Toryism formulated in the populist language of 'compulsive moralism'.[20] In contrast to this the *ideational-heritage* perspective saw Thatcherism in a longer historical perspective by demonstrating the long-standing existence of e.g. an economically liberal tendency within the party or even seeing Thatcherism as a continuation of traditional Conservative 'statescraft', i.e. a political strategy in which winning control of the centre of the political system by seeking electoral support wherever possible and trying to insulate this centre from external and domestic pressures.[21] From the perspective of policy change, it is, however, difficult to find academic analysts who claim that everything changed in the wake of 1979, and instead the dividing line in the literature runs between those who interpret the 1980s as a decade of *gradual revolution* in which the Conservative government reconstructed Britain on the basis of the general ideas identified by the strategic-revolution paradigm, gradually shifting political attention from macro-economics and industrial relations in the early 1980s toward the issues of privatisation and reform of the welfare state in the late 1980s.[22] Conversely, a more sceptical approach is in evidence in the *implementation-failure* perspective which tends to concentrate on the relationship between ideological principles and/or stated aims on the one hand, and implemented policies and their impact on the other. Here the overall impression is clearly one of very uneven progress, with reforms being attempted in some areas but delayed or eschewed in areas deemed to be politically dangerous, and resulting in outcomes that involve relatively limited change.[23]

As a specific Scottish initiative where a government-sponsored body was given responsibility for promoting economic development, the SDA would seem to be at odds with central Thatcherite principles, but again different interpretations can be found in the existing academic literature. Some authors have interpreted the history of the SDA in a way which can be summarised under the heading of *external revolution*, stressing that profound changes took place from 1975 to 1991 primarily as a result of external political pressure. From this perspective the Agency pursued an interventionist strategy in the early years, while the 1980s came to be dominated by strategies that worked with rather than against the market and favoured 'soft' policy instruments such as advisory services and network building instead of 'hard' policy instruments such as equity investment and subsidised industrial property – but despite this strategic compliance, the organisation had never been fully accepted politically and ultimately this paved the way for the adoption of the Scottish Enterprise proposal.[24] Contrary to this local, but quite radical, version of the gradual-revolution interpretation of Thatcherism, an alternative perspective on the development of the SDA can be encapsulated under the heading of *internal evolution* according to which individual policy areas – and indeed the overall policy profile of the Agency – changed through a predominantly incremental learning-by-doing process. According to this local version of the implementation-failure interpretation of Thatcherism, the early years are seen as less 'interventionist' in terms of strategies while at the same time it is stressed that the 1980s saw the continuation and development of activities that were clearly not in accordance with the liberal economic philosophy espoused by the Conservative government – and it is stressed that the Scottish Enterprise initiative only became government policy after a 'political maverick' bypassed the 'usual channels' of Scottish political governance.[25]

3. The SDA and Thatcher: A Game of Two Halves?
The previous section set the scene by introducing the institutional and political background for the encounter between the Thatcher government and the SDA. This section will focus on two critical junctions in the development of the organisation under the Conservatives: first the consequences of the change of government in 1979, and then the adoption of the *Scottish Enterprise* proposal which the Agency as a central actor in Scottish regional policy.

1979 and the SDA: Transformation or Symbolic Reconfiguration?

Having been elected in 1979, the new Conservative government made a public point of changing the guidelines directing SDA activities so that the organisation in the future was barred from acting as an interventionist body: no more should it be possible to use Agency funding to acquire controlling equity shares in private Scottish firms, the most important activity should henceforth be the attraction of foreign investment to Scotland, and all SDA policies should operate on a commercial basis so that the private sector was not subjected to unfair competition from a tax-financed public body.[26] After nearly a decade of Conservative sponsorship, an official government review concluded that the Agency's 'approach to economic development is consistent with present government philosophy',[27] and Scottish Industry Minister Ian Lang motivated continued support for the organisation by summarising its current role as 'working with the grain of our capitalist economy ... [as] an engine of free enterprise, creative and catalytic'.[28] Add these two public statements together and the impression is clearly one of a Conservative government successfully reshaping an interventionist Agency according to its own preferences,[29] but such an external-revolution interpretation does of course rest on the premise that radical change had indeed taken place. In the following four central aspects of SDA activities will be examined briefly in order to assess the extent and origins of change.

As the SDA was a semi-autonomous body operating at arm's-length of its political sponsors at the Scottish Office, great importance was always attached to the *corporate strategies* of the organisation,[30] and here a shift in tone and style is evident from the late 1970s to the late 1980s. In the early years the Agency occasionally talked about intervention and presented itself as the prime mover in economic renewal in Scotland, but after the change of government, 'enterprise' as a key word and the importance of working with the private sector – and only in areas where 'markets failed'– became much more prominent. At the same time, however, the continuities between the two periods are also obvious when looking in more detail at the key assumptions entailed in these statements about future SDA activities: 1) the nature of the regional problem was always defined in broad and potentially conflicting terms, employment and efficiency; 2) the main underlying value transforming inter-regional differences into legitimate objects of public policy was regional competitiveness rather than e.g. inter-regional equality or social stability; 3) the Agency emphatically distanced itself from rescues of ailing firms in the late 1970s, something which the Scottish Office investment guidelines only did after the change of government, and 4) the SDA was consistently cast as a subject in the process of regional development, while private firms were seen not only as objects of public policy but also as potential co-subjects even in the late 1970s. In short, it would seem to be difficult to identify a substantial change in SDA statements regarding its regional development strategies, although of course the changing rhetorical figures meant that the organisation could be construed as being associated with particular discursive positions and political trends. But despite these continuities in terms of the self-description of SDA intentions, the nature of individual activities and its overall profile may of course still have changed, and therefore it is necessary also to consider policies developed and implemented by the organisation,

By far the most controversial SDA activity was the industrial investment function which involved access to public venture capital for private firms on conditions defined by the Scottish Office but interpreted by the Agency with regard to prospects of viability regarding products, markets and management. If this activity had indeed been 'Thatcherised', then it would be expected that the overall level of activity was reduced in the 1980s compared to the 1970s, the firms targeted would shift from existing firms in traditional industries towards new firms in modern industries, investments would be assessed on increasingly commercial criteria, and the influence of the Agency on invested firms reduced. These claims can be assessed on the basis of in-depth interviews with investment staff about operating procedures, and by drawing on a purpose-built database covering key aspects of all major Agency investments undertaken from 1975 to 31 March 1990 and incorporating unpublished SDA data.[31]

With regard to the level of activity, the relative prominence of the investment function remained stable, accounting for *circa* 12 per cent of SDA gross expenditure, except for a brief period in the early 1980s,[32] and, as can be seen from Figure 1, activity was on a considerably higher level in the 1980s than in the 1970s both measured in real term expenditure and in the number of investments undertaken. Furthermore, while the characteristics of the invested firms did change, it was only in the second half of the 1980s that modern industries (electronics, biotechnology and services) accounted for around 50 per cent while prior to 1985 traditional Scottish industries – engineering, textiles, and food processing – made up more than 75 per cent of all investments undertaken and continued to be prominent even in the late 1980s. Similarly, while the importance of investment in new firms rose from *circa* 20 per cent to *circa* 50 per cent of the total number of investments since the late 1970s, investments that refinanced existing productive capacity (additional working capital, management buy-outs, etc.) have continuously accounted for more than 40 per cent of the total. Whether the industrial investment function did indeed become more commercial in its dealings with individual firms in the 1980s can be illuminated by focusing on those firms in which the involvement of the SDA was eventually terminated, either because the receiver had to be called in when a firm failed to perform adequately, or because stakes in more successful firm was sold to private investors. On both accounts the contrast between the 1970s and the 1980s is, however, not conclusive: the financial liabilities incurred by the SDA through less successful investments remained fairly stable around *circa* 10 per cent of the value of the portfolio until the late 1980s,[33] and while receipts from sales and repayments did increase significantly after the change of government, culminating in 1981/82 and again in the late 1980s,[34] this does not necessarily imply a more commercial approach on part of the development body, because when the SDA and the private sector knew that there was a strong political demand for sell-offs, this could easily depress prices and make it attractive for private investors to acquire even firms with a less convincing track record. Finally, the influence of the SDA on its invested firms has been affected by two trends. On the one hand the structure of the portfolio changed in the 1980s because the size of the average investment was cut by 75 per cent in order to spread the risk and increase private co-investment,[35] something which effectively precluded SDA control of individual companies. On the other hand the way in which the Agency tried to improve the performance of the invested firm changed: instead of providing direct managerial assistance by secondment *after* the investment has been undertaken, more stringent procedures for the evaluation of proposed projects *prior* to investing were introduced.[36] How these changes affected the SDA's ability to influence the actions of the private sector is, however, less obvious, because while the Agency's direct control of individual firms had always been limited – it was only in the first two years of operation that the Agency had acquired a small number of subsidiaries which by 1979 constituted only 22% of its invested firms[37] – reliance on private sector co-investment may in fact have enhanced the impact of its investments,[38] that is, of course, *if* the financial commitments of the SDA have been crucial in making marginal projects go ahead, and *if* the Agency's conditions for co-investing have significantly improved the proposed projects. All in all the implementation of investment function can hardly be said to have been radically changed, despite the new guidelines issued by the Conservative government in 1980, and the most remarkable change identified – reliance on minority investments – may have been off-set by new and more stringent appraisal procedures that maintained or even enhanced public sector influence over firms within the Scottish economy. But then the latter were low-key activities that were not heavily publicised, unlike a number of high-profile failures of firms controlled by the Agency in the late 1970s, or indeed the new 1980 guidelines, and thus the development of the industrial investment function could still be construed as as a case of 'Thatcherisation'.

Table 2: Indexes of SDA Investment Activity
(Source: Calculated on the basis of SDAINV and SDA 1977-1991)

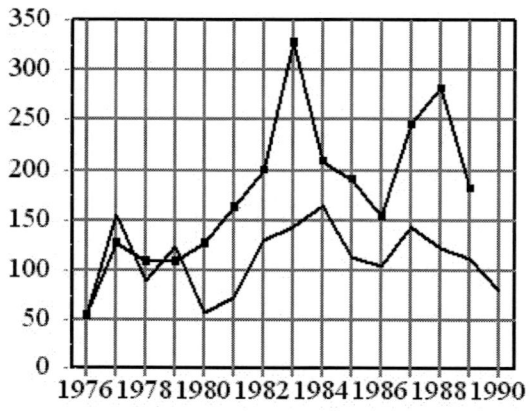

→ New HOID invested firms
— Total gross expenditure

100 = average 1976-1979, real term expenditure figures relate to financial years, investment projects to calendar years.

In most other areas of SDA policy a similar picture can be found where continuity or incremental change dominate, where many changes enhance rather than dilute the influence of public actors on the strategies of private firms, and where the arm's-length organisation maintains a proactive role *vis-à-vis* the reactive regulators at the Scottish Office. Efforts to attract *inward investment* to Scotland were increased in the 1980s, but this trend had started already before the change of government, and the organisational platform for this – a joint body where the Agency's promotional and sectoral expertise joint forces with the grant-giving powers of the Scottish Office – operated as part of the SDA and became increasingly proactive and selective in its activities, i.e. public actors deciding which private firms to approach with investment proposals.[39] Both with regard to *advisory services* and *sectoral initiatives* the 1980s saw expansion of activities in ways that would not seem to reflect priorities of the Thatcher government: while pre-1979 initiatives focused mainly on small firms and high-tech industries, new developments in the 1980s also included large firms in traditional sectors, and again activities became more and more proactive and selective, with the Agency deciding which groups of firms should be given priority.[40] The only major possible exception from this pattern would appear to be in *property provision* where the emphasis of the spatially targeted initiatives shifted from areas of industrial closures towards city centre development, and a significant part of the SDA's factory portfolio was sold off to private investors in the late 1980. Although both of these changes would seem to be in accordance with Thatcherite thinking – giving priority to new areas of economic activity and privatisation of public assets – the overall picture was rather more complex. On the one hand some of the largest image-oriented city-centre developments by the Agency had been initiated before the change of government, despite Tory attempts to take full credit for e.g. the Scottish Exhibition and Conference Centre. On the other hand the severely delayed relinquishing of the SDA's role as 'Scotland's biggest industrial landlord' only affected the organisation's administrative role as property administrator but did not prevent it from building new facilities in support of economic development within the region.[41]

In short, policy area by policy area changes strengthened rather than reduced the potential influence of public priorities in the regional economy from the late 1970s to the early 1990s, and in parallel with this the balance of the SDA's activity profile also shifted in the same direction,[42] so that all in all policy changes would seem to run counter to liberal ideological preferences, making even a 'gradualist external revolution' interpretation difficult to sustain. This did of course not prevent either Conservative ministers or their opponents from claiming that the original approach of the SDA had been that of 'an overarching Agency controlling the economy' and 'protecting ailing companies',[43] or, conversely, that in the 1980s the new-style 'commercial' and 'catalytic' approach was an attempt to 'out-Thatcher Thatcher'[44] – not just because of the adversarial nature of British politics, but also because of the existence of enough similarities between SDA corporate discourse and government political rhetoric to make this appear entirely plausible.

From Agency to Enterprise: Thatcherism Strikes Back?
Not long after two positive reviews of the SDA in 1987 which had seen both ministers and civil servants endorse the achievements of the organisation, Bill Hughes, chairman of the Confederation of British Industry (CBI) in Scotland, proposed a merger of the Agency with the Scottish arm of the Training Agency. Circumventing the Scottish Office and obtaining the public support of the Prime Minister in September 1988, the proposal for creation

of a two-tier network of RDAs consisting of a strategic national core and a network of Local Enterprise Companies swiftly became official government policy, and on the first of April 1991 the SDA had ceased to exist and the merged entity, Scottish Enterprise, began to operate. Although combining development of firms and human resources and decentralising policy delivery could have obvious advantages, the initiative was generally seen as having a strong party-political dimension: was this not an attempt by Thatcherites, dissatisfied with their apparent inability to control the activities of an inherited arm's-length organisation, to exorcise the ghost of Labour interventionism by refashioning Scottish regional policy in a more palatable form?[45]

In order to disentangle the politics of regional policy in Scotland in the 1980s, it is important to understand the position of the main political parties both before and after the change of government in 1979. Although the major parties continued to agree about a preferential regionalist approach to Scottish economic development – Scotland had 'special needs' which legitimised special/additional measures compared to e.g. the equally crisis-ridden North-East England – what this consensus about territorial politics should mean in practice looked increasingly uncertain by the beginning of 1979: the Labour government seemed somewhat impatient with the speed at which the SDA moved, while the Conservative opposition reiterated their intention to maintain the SDA but also promised what was presented as a major revamp of its controversial industrial investment function, suspected of being a vehicle of back-door nationalisation and for giving unfair advantages to its invested firms. Although the precise meaning of political demands for 'more proactivity' or 'more commercial investments' remained unclear, the SDA was likely to face pressures to adjust its activities no matter which party had won the general election, and after the Conservatives had formed the government they did what they had promised during the election campaign, namely retain the SDA with revised guidelines for the industrial investment function, insisting on the importance of private sector co-investment. In terms of policy implementation this merely strengthened existing trends within the Agency, and the real significance of the new guidelines was political, namely to serve as a symbolic marker of change having happened and thereby effectively reduced the role of the public-private dimension in future debate about the SDA. After the anxieties of the first months under the new government caused by rattling of sabres by radical elements in the governing party, the arm's-length body was for the next eight years largely left to 'get on with it' by Scottish Office ministers happy to be associated with the positive publicity from e.g. inward investment attraction or redevelopment of derelict industrial sites – a period in which the main source of external influence on Agency activities came from civil servants in the sponsor department worried about the extensive discretion which had been vested in the arm's-length body. In short, the early 1980s saw the political discourse of the Conservative government reinterpret the meaning of the SDA: any notion of state intervention or public enterprise disappeared, and instead the Agency was presented as an organisation that in the words of the newly elected Prime Minister Thatcher could help by 'easing the transition from the industries and jobs of the past, to the industries and jobs of the future'[46] while Scottish Office ministers used its visible high-profile activities to signal that the Scottish Tories remained within the long-standing preferential regionalist consensus about Scotland having specific needs that required special, additional, Scottish measures.

So if the Scottish Conservatives had generally found the SDA and its activities agreeable and useful, how can we then understand what appears to be a sudden change of heart taking place in less than a year from 1987 to 1988? The Thatcherite ideological connotations derived from the name and the personal intervention of the Prime Minister were of course important as an enabling factor, but the timing of the Scottish Enterprise proposal – shortly after fulsome political endorsements of the SDA in 1987 – would seem to suggest that interpreting the merger as the product of a longstanding ideological distrust is, at best, a rather incomplete view. Instead other political considerations seem to have been more important, including short-term ones relating to ministerial self-advancement by comprehensively wrong-footing the opposition - improving training was supported by the trade unions and decentralised policy implementation by local authorities dominated by the Labour councillors – but, more important, perhaps, was more strategic considerations such as adding a sizeable policy area like training to the responsibilities of the Scottish Office, a clear instance of preferential regionalism which put a new and rather different perspective on Thatcher's words about Scottish Enterprise as 'a Scottish solution to respond to Scottish needs'.[47] Moreover, this could be achieved in a manner that could be presented as increasing the accountability of public policy to the local business community while at the same time allegedly doing little damage to the existing policies of the Agency, although some disquiet was expressed by the loss of strategic direction if 'the national core' of the new two-tier quango ended up being too small and specialist staff responsible for e.g. sectoral networks or advanced advisory services were dispersed throughout the new Local Enterprise Companies. Despite having been a front-runner in regional policy innovation through the SDA, not just in the UK but also from a wider European perspective, the politics of regional policy in Scotland would not seem to have changed much from the 1970s to the early 1990s: preferential regionalism continued to be the shared starting point, and thus creating visible results, either through tangible policy measures or organisational change, remained crucial in party-political contestations.

4. The SDA, Scottish Conservatism and Preferential Regionalism

Looked at as a case study of pre-devolution governance in Scotland, the meeting between the SDA and the Thatcher governments suggests conclusions along two, partly complementary, lines.

On the one hand the analysis clearly showed that political authority was still embodied in the Prime Minister, ultimately situated in London, even with regard to specific issues such as the institutional set-up in low-politics areas of public policy such as regional development and training. The personal support lend by Margaret Thatcher to the Scottish Enterprise proposal was obviously important in securing momentum for what might otherwise have been one of the more curious ideas in the 1988 silly season, but as the working out in detail of the new way of doing things was handled within the Scottish territorial politics network, the result was something which – apart from the new brand name – looked more like a take-over by the SDA of the Scottish operation of the British Training Agency than a termination of what used to be one of Europe's most prominent RDAs.[48]

On the other hand, the analysis would at the same time also seem to lend support to the importance of, if not a 'Scottish political system' then certainly a territorial policy network revolving around the Scottish Office and its associated bodies. At the parliamentary level the fact that Scotland had its own cabinet minister gave the prevailing pragmatic (non-Thatcherite) views among Scottish Tories added weight: the Prime Minister's favourite ideologue Keith Joseph, industry secretary in the first Thatcher government, was clearly sceptical about the merits of regional policy in general and regional development agencies in particular, while the politics of the long-serving Scottish secretary George Younger were clearly much more in line with traditional One-Nation Toryism. At the administrative level the Industry Department of the Scottish Office clearly had a strong sense of ownership – something that many Agency executives saw as undue interference in day-to-day routines – which meant that top civil servants would routinely defend the advantages of having an arm's-length body and even its main the principles of operation in face of hostile political questioning. Moreover, as an organisation with a separate corporate identity and the ability to exercise initiative and cultivate the public at large, the SDA was able to present itself as enjoying some degree of autonomy from the whims and strings of ministers and civil servants – presenting itself as taking a long-term professional view of regional development – and hence able to gain support from members of the business community, something which was an invaluable political asset in a decade where businessmen were trumpeted as role models and the embodiment of social virtue. And finally the concept of special treatment for Scotland through the SDA and its activities was hardly thinkable without the existence of preferential regionalism as a consensual assumption underlying Scottish political debate and, albeit sometimes grudgingly, accepted at the British level.

Add these two conclusions together and the introduction of devolution would be likely to make some difference to the governance of Scotland. On the one hand Scottish decision-making about Scottish affairs was likely to increase because devolved areas of public policy would be insulated from direct intervention from London. On the other hand the persistent need for some degree of policy coordination within the UK was likely to imply that the Scottish freedom of manoeuvre would probably not have changed as much as both proponents and opponents of constitutional reform have tended to claim. This is the history of *Scottish Enterprise*, and it still remains to be written.

Notes

[1] Michael Keating, *Nations against the State. The New Politics of Nationalism in Quebec, Catalonia and Scotland* (London: Macmillan 1996) p. 168.
[2] James G. Kellas, *The Scottish Political System*, 4th Ed. (Cambridge: Cambridge UP 1989).
[3] Alice Brown, David McCrone, and Lindsay Paterson, *Politics and Society in Scotland* (Houndmills: Macmillan, 1996) p. 15.
[4] Mike Danson, Greg Lloyd, and David Newlands, "'Scottish Enterprise'; Towards a Model Agency or a Flawed Initiative?" *Regional Studies* 23 (1989).
[5] Chris Moore and Simon Booth, *Managing Competition. Meso-Corporatism, Pluralism, and the Negotiated Order in Scotland* (Oxford: Clarendon 1989).
[6] For a longer version of this argument, including discussions of an institutionalist approach to the study of regional policy and governance, see Henrik Halkier, *Institutions, Discourse and Regional Development. The Scottish Development Agency and the Politics of Regional Policy* (Brussels: PIE Peter Lang 2006).
[7] S. Rokkan and D. Urwin, *Economy, Territory, Identity: Politics of West European Peripheries* (London: Sage 1983).
[8] See Lindsay Paterson, *The Autonomy of Modern Scotland* (Edinburgh: Edinburgh UP 1994) Ch. 3.

[9] Kellas, *The Scottish Political System*, 4th Ed. Ch. 3.
[10] Arthur; Keating Midwinter, Michael; Mitchell, James, *Politics and Public Policy in Scotland* (Houndmills: Macmillan 1991) Ch. 4.
[11] Brown, McCrone, and Paterson, *Politics and Society in Scotland* Ch. 3. Midwinter, *Politics and Public Policy in Scotland* pp. 75ff.
[12] Kellas, *The Scottish Political System*, 4th Ed. Ch. 5
[13] Brown, McCrone, and Paterson, *Politics and Society in Scotland* pp. 177ff, Robert C. Thomsen, *Selves and Others of Political Nationalism in Stateless Nations: National Identity-Building Processes in the Modern Histories of Scotland and Newfoundland* (PhD Thesis: Department of English, University of Aarhus, 2001) Ch. 4.
[14] Paterson, *The Autonomy of Modern Scotland* pp. 112ff.
[15] I. G. C. Hutchison, *Scottish Politics in the Twentieth Century* (Houndmills: Macmillan 1999) pp. 122ff.
[16] ""It Is His Oil" Poster," (Edinburgh: SNP, 1974).
[17] Halkier, *Institutions, Discourse and Regional Development. The Scottish Development Agency and the Politics of Regional Policy* Ch. 5.
[18] Bob Jessop et al., *Thatcherism. A Tale of Two Nations* (Cambridge: Polity 1988) pp. 221ff.
[19] Eric J. Evans, *Thatcher and Thatcherism* (London: Routledge, 1997), Andrew Gamble, *The Free Economy and the Strong State: The Politics of Thatcherism* (Houndmills: Macmillan, 1988), E. H. H. Green, *Ideologies of Conservatism. Conservative Political Ideas in the 20th Century* (Oxford: Oxford UP 2002).
[20] E.g. Gamble, *The Free Economy and the Strong State: The Politics of Thatcherism*, Stuart Hall and Martin Jacques, eds., *The Politics of Thatcherism* (London: Lawrence & Wishart, 1983), Jessop et al., *Thatcherism. A Tale of Two Nations*.
[21] E.g. Jim Bulpitt, *Territory and Power in the Uk* (Manchester: Manchester UP 1983), Green, *Ideologies of Conservatism. Conservative Political Ideas in the 20th Century*.
[22] E.g. Ron Martin, "The Political Economy of Britain's North-South Divide," *Transactions of the Institute of British Geographers NS* 13 (1988), Peter Riddell, *The Thatcher Era. And Its Legacy* (Oxford: Blackwell 1991).
[23] E.g. Brendan Evans, *Thatcherism and British Politics, 1975-1999* (Stroud: Sutton 1999), Jens Peter Frølund Thomsen, *Governing against Pressure. State British Politics and Trade Unions in the 1980s: Governing against Pressure* (Aldershot: Dartmouth 1996), James I. Walsh, "When Do Ideas Matter? Explaining the Successes and Failures of Thatcherite Ideas," *Comparative Political Studies* 33, no. 4 (2000).
[24] Danson, Lloyd, and Newlands, "'Scottish Enterprise'; Towards a Model Agency or a Flawed Initiative?", Gordon MacLeod, "The Cult of Enterprise in a Networked, Learning Region? Governing Business and Skills in Lowland Scotland," *Regional Studies* 30, no. 8 (1996).
[25] William Lever and Chris Moore, eds., *The City in Transition. Policies and Agencies for the Regeneration of Clydeside* (Oxford: Clarendon, 1986), Chris Moore, "The Hughes Initiative: The Blueprint for Enterprise?" *Local Economy* 3, no. 4 (1989), Moore and Booth, *Managing Competition. Meso-Corporatism, Pluralism, and the Negotiated Order*

in Scotland.

26 "SDA - Industrial Investment Guidelines," (Edinburgh: SEPD 1980).
27 "1986 Review of the Sda. Report of the Review Group to the Secretary of State for Scotland," (Edinburgh: IDS, 1987), quotes pp. III, 24.
28 *House of Commons Parliamentary Debates* 21.10.87 vol. 120 cols. 839ff.
29 The basic argument in e.g. Mike Danson, Greg Lloyd, and David Newlands, "Scottish Enterprise: An Evolving Approach to Integrating Economic Development in Scotland," *The Scottish Government Yearbook* 1990 (1990).
30 Halkier, *Institutions, Discourse and Regional Development. The Scottish Development Agency and the Politics of Regional Policy* Ch. 7.
31 Ibid. Ch. 8.
32 Calculated on the basis of "Annual Report," (Glasgow: SDA 1977-91).
33 Calculated on the basis of Ibid.
34 Calculated on the basis of Ibid.
35 Calculated on the basis of SDAINV and Ibid.
36 Interviews with SDA Investment Director Donald Patience 31.5.90, and Head of SDA's Industry Services Division Gerry Murray 30.7.90.
37 Calculated on the basis of SDAINV.
38 This is, not surprisingly, maintained by the Agency (interview Investment Director Donald Patience 31.5.90) and the Scottish Office (IDS 1987, pp. 45ff).
39 Halkier, *Institutions, Discourse and Regional Development. The Scottish Development Agency and the Politics of Regional Policy* Ch. 10.
40 Ibid. Ch.s 9, 11.
41 Ibid. Ch. 12.
42 Expenditure on industrial investment and information-based services not only grew nearly 160% in absolute terms from 1979 to 1991, but these areas also increased their share of total Agency spending from 14% to 37% (Calculated on the basis of SDA 1980-91).
43 Quotes by SDA Chief Executive George Mathewson 9.7.90, and Head of the SDA Policy Unit Frank Kirwan 1.6.90.
44 Danson, Lloyd, and Newlands, "'Scottish Enterprise'; Towards a Model Agency or a Flawed Initiative?" p. 562.
45 For an extended version of this argument, see Halkier, *Institutions, Discourse and Regional Development. The Scottish Development Agency and the Politics of Regional Policy* Ch. 14.
46 Margaret Thatcher, *Complete Public Statements, 1945-90* (Oxford: Oxford UP 1999) Speech to the Scottish Conservative Conference 12.5.79.
47 Ibid. Speech to the Scottish CBI 8.9.88.
48 For an early assesment, see Henrik Halkier, "New Lamps for Old? The Industrial Strategies of Scottish Enterprise," *Quarterly Economic Commentary* 17, no. 4 (1992).

BEYOND THE CRINGE: SCOTTISH NATIONALISM SINCE THE 1960s

Robert C. Thomsen

Abstract

A popular and political nationalist movement arose in Scotland in the 1960s and was strengthened in the following decade by the discovery of North Sea oil. Nevertheless, in 1979 large sections of the electorate abandoned the idea of self-government on referendum day. Critics blamed centuries of well-rehearsed inferiority – the 'Scottish cringe'. Developments in the 1980s and 1990s in the cultural, political and civic spheres brought about a more determined and widespread nationalism. By the time of the 1997 referendum, the 'cringe' had been firmly replaced by consensus and confidence – causing a massive 'yes' vote and, consequently, the re-establishment of the Scottish parliament in Edinburgh.

When, in 1707, the Scottish parliament voted to abolish itself, it would be 292 years before a Scottish parliament would again sit in Edinburgh. The parliament that opened in 1999 would be a very different institution, democratically elected and with different powers, but it would nevertheless be seen by most Scots as the successful culmination of a long struggle to restore self-government to Scotland. The rhetoric used in this connection spoke of the 're-opening' of the Scottish parliament, making the direct link to the political status of national independence before 1707.

The new parliament can certainly be said to owe its existence to politically expressed nationalism, but it is a nationalism which is often considered to have been 'belated'; at least compared to nationalist movements in other small European nations, whose struggles for national sovereignty were mostly nineteenth-century phenomena. In the Scottish case, in contrast, nationalism until the 1960s expressed itself mainly in a non-political fashion: celebrating the romantic past and unique culture of a people, but rarely making any political demands for constitutional change on the basis of it. Critics have blamed this lack of 'real' nationalism – or as Tom Nairn famously labelled it: 'cultural sub-nationalism'[1] – on the conscious decision of Scottish middleclass power-holders not to rock the British imperial boat that provided so well for a country that would otherwise sink into poverty, and on a general sense of inferiority, particularly in relation to English history and culture.

The latter has been described by various scholars, journalists and politicians as the 'Scottish cringe'. In 2004, for example, Scotland's First Minister Jack McConnell, speaking to the Scottish Labour conference, said: 'Poverty of ambition and poverty of expectation is the most damaging poverty of all [...]. I want to end the Scottish cringe'.[2]

Political nationalism comes in many forms, from demands for a degree of home rule to separatism, and as such was certainly an aspect of the home rule movement in the 1880s and 1910s. Political nationalism was also a feature of Scottish party politics since 1928, when the National Party of Scotland, later the Scottish National Party (SNP), was established. Still, the kind of political nationalism that would seriously challenge 'the cringe' would only come later. The rise in the percentage of Scots supporting constitutional options other than the status quo indicates the increasing popularity of political nationalism in the post-World War II period. In 1945, in the first poll of its kind in Scotland, only 8 per cent of respondents claimed to be in favour of Scottish independence, while 53 per cent favoured devolution. In the period 1965 to 1974, in comparison, the average in favour of independence hovered around 22 per cent, with the devolution option preferred by an average of 63 per cent.[3] Another significant change occurred with an increase in support for the SNP.

First wave: the 1960s and 1970s
In 1967 the SNP won 200,000 votes and 69 seats in the local elections as well as the previously safe Labour seat of Hamilton in a by-election. In the elections and by-elections of the decade following Hamilton, the nationalists enjoyed increasing, although not constant support from Scots: their share of the Scottish vote went from 5 per cent in 1966 to 11.4 per cent in 1970, to 21.9 per cent in February 1974 and 30.4 per cent in October 1974. Several political and economic developments in the period following 1945 would come to be significant to the perception of Scotland's position within the UK, and together they explain the sudden increase in support for constitutional change and the SNP. Of particular importance are the decline of the British Empire, industry and economy generally, and Scottish economic recession specifically. The Wilson, Heath and Callaghan administrations found themselves in a series of economic crises with a negative effect on the quality of life in Britain. As the foundations of the British welfare state were being gradually eroded, being ruled from Westminster came to appear to be much less of a bargain. Since the Beveridge Report, the idea of the welfare state had been embraced by the Scots, not least because Scotland was often more in need of welfare benefits than other parts of the UK. Many Scots now

came to share the perception that changing governments were failing to deliver according to the social contract, which had hitherto been such a powerful unifying incentive.

There existed in Scotland at the time a sense of relative deprivation with regard not only to other small European societies, but also to England. Scotland was ridden by high unemployment rates and general socio-economic malaise while other parts of the UK were seen to prosper, at least relatively. Hitherto, insensitive Conservative administrations could be blamed, and their regimes waited out, but in the late 1960s it was becoming clear that even Labour would not necessarily be able to deliver: unemployment rose to new heights and in spite of its promises the Wilson Government did not appear to be doing anything to ease Scotland's problems.

In this light, support for the SNP in the late 1960s can be explained partly as a form of protest. Labour ceased to be able to translate Scottish discontent into Labour support. It is not coincidental, however, that the choice of party became the SNP and the cause chosen became the national cause. A strong sense of Scotland as a distinct nation with special needs had survived since the eighteenth century – as witnessed in the nineteenth-century home rule movement and the Scottish Covenant of the late 1940s. However, had these negative incentives not come about, and had either of the two major parties seriously entertained the idea of home rule, it is doubtful whether the SNP would have had the same amount of success in channelling a general appreciation for the idea of Scottish self-government into support for its more radical, separatist agenda in the late 1960s.

In his May 1968 'Declaration of Perth' Edward Heath had shocked the Scottish Conservatives by announcing Tory support for a Scottish Assembly. The party, however, made no serious attempt at establishing such an assembly. At their 1973 conference, the largely unenthusiastic Conservatives voted not to speed up the process of establishing a Scottish Assembly, and the idea of devolution was in essence rejected in favour of a policy of local government reform.[4] Labour, as we shall see, embraced devolution from 1974, but not whole-heartedly.

North Sea oil and 'civic' nationalism
True to the nature of protests movements, political nationalism, as expressed in support for the SNP, was showing signs of fatigue already by 1970. The nationalist vote continued to increase but at a much slower pace and in local elections support was declining. This might well have been the beginning of a weary journey for the political nationalist movement had not new additional incentives appeared. First, there was a further decline of

socio-economic conditions in the UK and in Scotland, and second – and most importantly – oil entered the nationalist equation. Oil was discovered off the North Sea coast of Scotland in November 1970, and coinciding with Britain's severe socio-economic crisis, it offered to Scots, in historian Michael Lynch's words: 'the prospect of escape from their dependence on the new, lesser Britain'.[5] Forecasts rose quickly and as oil prices were on a steady rise, oil indeed promised to make Scotland a wealthy, possibly even independent society.

The SNP leadership made good use of what they saw as an economic alternative to the UK, and the new resource soon became a powerful weapon in the nationalist struggle. The SNP slogan of the 1960s, 'Put Scotland First', was replaced by the highly successful 'It's Scotland's Oil' (1972) and its follow-up: 'Rich Scots or Poor Britons' (1974). The SNP 1974 General Election manifestos accentuated the oil discoveries and their prospects for Scotland. The main idea presented was that '[t]he enormous wealth of the oil and gas fields off the Scottish coast, allied to our other vast resources, offers ever-improving living standards to the people of Scotland – <u>when they demand a Scottish Government</u>'.[6] Increasingly, the unionist argument that Scotland would never be able to make it alone lost a great deal of its appeal, and the SNP managed to reach out to a larger number of Scots than ever before; probably because many voters who had not previously prioritised national issues now had an economic incentive to do so. In the October 1974 General Election the party increased its share of the vote to 30.4 per cent. There can be little doubt that the renewed impetus that political nationalism enjoyed through increased support for the SNP owed a great deal to the positive oil prospects of the day.

Of further interest to the student of Scottish nationalism in this period is the fact that the two dominant and interrelated themes in SNP manifestos were socio-economic considerations and a lack of democracy/political influence. This left little or no space in SNP rhetoric in the 1970s for what might be termed ethno-cultural matters. Ethnicity remains implied in references to, for instance, 'the Scottish people', but emphasis on the survival of national culture and identity – a basic element in most traditional nationalist movements – is rare. Because ethno-cultural matters generally remain a supportive rather than a causal element, Scottish political nationalism has often been labelled 'civic' (as opposed to 'ethnic').[7]

Labour and the 1979 referendum
The Labour Party had been in favour of home rule for periods of the first half of the century, but by the mid-1950s had committed itself to unionism.

It took the February 1974 General Election to seriously change the mind of the Labour leadership. Riding on a wave of oil and protest votes, the modernised SNP won 21.9 per cent of the Scottish vote. The Labour Party, seeing its very important and formerly safe Scottish seats threatened, was forced to re-introduce the old Labour policy of home rule to its manifesto. Labour's U-turn on devolution can thus be interpreted as a result of a highly pragmatic choice made by the Labour leadership in London for tactical political reasons. The new policy was now introduced to the public within weeks of the October 1974 General Election.

Labour remained in support of devolution throughout the 1970s, which turned out to be crucial to the development of political nationalism in Scotland. Firstly, political nationalism of a decidedly devolutionist, rather than a separatist nature, had now placed itself firmly on the political agenda. Secondly, nationalist sentiment from the mid-1970s was no longer measurable only or even mainly by support for the SNP. Thirdly, devolution became so closely associated with Labour policies that the success or failure of the party spelled the success or failure of Scottish devolution.

In 1975 the Labour government produced a white paper on devolution, which would eventually form the basis of the 1978 Scotland Act, to be laid out for a consultative referendum in 1979. The legislative and administrative powers of the proposed assembly would include some aspects of health, social welfare, education, housing, local government, transport, physical planning, agriculture and fisheries, and the legal system.

All major Scottish newspapers, including the until recently unionist *Glasgow Herald*, along with all political parties, except for the Conservatives, supported Scottish home rule in the Spring of 1979. In spite of high expectations for the 1979 referendum, and as a big surprise to politicians and media alike, the seemingly unstoppable march of political nationalism in Scotland came to an abrupt halt on 1 March that year. What should have been a landmark in the history of political nationalism in Scotland, the establishment of a Scottish Assembly, failed to materialise as only 32.9 per cent of the electorate chose to endorse such a move in the referendum. Although this constituted a majority of all votes cast (51.6 per cent), this was far below the mark of 40 per cent of the electorate required for any change to take place.

Ever since the failed referendum, politicians, scholars and others have discussed possible reasons for what appeared to be this sudden decline in support for nationalism in Scotland. A factor which many analysts credit with the major responsibility for the outcome of the 1979 referendum was the close association of the Scotland Act with the image of the Labour government. 1978-79 had been the 'Winter of Discontent' with massive labour dissatisfaction and strikes in the public sector, and the failure of the Labour government that this represented was invariably associated with the devolution proposal it had developed. Labour, it was becoming clear, was losing its grip on power, and the devolution scheme could be seen as just another desperate attempt at saving votes. In addition, Labour was far from united on the issue, and thus its campaign was less than convincing. In fact, the entire 'Yes' side was divided. The SNP had agreed to support the Assembly in 1975 but Labour refused to be part of the 'Yes' campaign along with them.

The fact that Scotland could at this point be seen to be improving its relative economic position within the UK might have persuaded some Scots that Westminster, rather than an inexperienced Edinburgh assembly, would be better equipped to get Scotland out of the socio-economic morass it found itself in. In the minds of most Scots – middle class Scots in particular – a viable alternative to full membership of the UK did not exist; North Sea oil was turning out not to provide the bonanza expected in the early part of the decade. Many factors combined into a widespread lack of confidence in Scotland's ability to do better as a more autonomous entity within the UK. In the following decade, the Scottish cringe inferiority complex was often used to explain both the 'belatedness' of political nationalism and the failure of the 1979 referendum.[8]

Although of some importance, the Scottish cringe is a factor whose power should not be overestimated. The failure of the 1979 referendum to produce self-government for Scotland was a combination of several factors: the 'Yes' side was divided at all levels, and carried the stigma of failed government. Also, for the first time in recent history Scotland had climbed a rung on the socio-economic ladder to become one of the relatively well-off parts of the UK. With the oil bubble burst, there seemed to be no better alternative to economic dependence on the UK.

Re-building momentum: the 1980s and 1990s
After 1979, Scottish political nationalism found itself in a serious crisis. For those nationalists who had endorsed the Scotland Act, the 1979 referendum marked a traumatic turn in their fortune that it would take some time to recover from. Several new factors combined, however, to make the nationalist movement of the 1980s and 1990s of an even stronger nature than the one which characterised the 1960s and 1970s.

Thatcherism and the democratic deficit

As conditions of Scottish industry and the general socio-economic situation declined again during the last two decades of the twentieth century, dissatisfaction with this state of affairs fostered a growing sense in Scotland of neglect by Westminster – of having been made increasingly peripheral by indifferent British governments led by Conservative Prime Ministers Margaret Thatcher and John Major. A 1993 poll for the *Herald* showed that 70 per cent of the Scots agreed that 'Scotland had been worse treated than other parts of the UK'.[9] Scottish anti-Tory sentiment in this period is well illustrated by the history of the Conservative vote in Scotland, which declined from 31.4 per cent in 1979 to 17.5 per cent in 1997.

After taking power in 1979, the Thatcher government set out to alter the British welfare state radically, and these alterations, affecting mainly health and education, combined with policies of centralisation to quickly alienate large sections of the Scottish population. Scottish institutions which had become carriers of a distinct Scottish identity, such as the nationalised industries, the education system, local government and the churches, fell victims to Margaret Thatcher's policies. Many of these actors in what can be defined loosely as 'civil society' thus felt the brunt of Conservative neo-liberal policies and therefore, in the 1980s, were seen to move in large numbers into the devolutionist camp. Furthermore, Scotland suffered the indignity of being used as a guinea-pig for the notorious 'poll tax' – opposed almost universally in Scotland by everyone outwith the Conservative Party. The common perception was that the Conservatives had made the deliberate decision to target that part of the British Isles called Scotland, and this galvanised support for political nationalism among a growing number of Scots.

In addition, a perception of a democratic deficit caused by the present constitutional set-up was underlined by the fact that although most Scots voted for parties other than the Conservatives (supported by only about one in five), that party continued to form the government throughout the 1980s and for most of the 1990s.

Such circumstances help explain why opinion polls in the period from 1979 to 1989 show a steady support for home rule at about 50 per cent of respondents, as well as an increase in support for the independence option (from 7 per cent to 34 per cent), indicating a radicalisation of political nationalism in Scotland in this period. By 1992, the almost universal rejection by the Scots of Conservative neo-liberal policies moved David McCrone to declare: 'We're all nationalists now'.[10]

Europe, the new viable alternative

Due mainly to a collapse of oil prices from the mid-1980s, North Sea oil came to be seen less and less as a viable alternative to economic dependence of the UK. In its place, an increasingly positive incentive to political nationalism in the 1980s and 1990s came to be the European Community/ European Union which, through its structural funds, was providing economic assistance to troubled regional economies, making e.g. Ireland the economic 'tiger' of the western world. Scottish political nationalists, particularly in the SNP, now looked to Ireland and imagined the success story repeating itself with Scotland at its centre. From an early stand of fierce opposition to the EC, by 1989 the SNP had accomplished a complete U-turn on the question of EU membership. The SNP was now convinced of the benefits of European integration and saw it as the springboard for a new kind of 'Independence in Europe'.[11] The picture which was now being painted placed the Scots between an old malfunctioning union and a new progressive one.

Along with the SNP, many Scots who had previously felt reluctant to risk political and thus economic dependence on the UK now had in the EU a real alternative, a life-line which would assure that a greater measure of autonomy would not result in socio-economic misery. Scotland became the more EU-positive part of the UK (or at least less critical), and EU membership remains a factor to take into consideration with regard to the development of Scottish nationalism in this period.

Labour, the new standard bearer

The Labour Party was effectively shut out from political power from 1979 to 1997 and consequently had to seek other means of political influence. One vista was to attempt to rekindle the home rule fires in Scotland and Wales, and by the late 1980s Scottish Labour had made the conversion from unionist party in the early 1970s to fully convinced devolutionist party.

Since Labour returned to a policy of devolution, political nationalism in Scotland ceased to be measurable only by support for the SNP. A 1991 survey correlating identity with voting behaviour found that 44 per cent of Labour voters compared with 51 per cent of SNP voters, 27 per cent of Conservative voters and 21 per cent of Liberal Democrat voters defined themselves as 'Scottish, not British'.[12] Taking the difference in size of voting groups into consideration, more Labour voters than SNP voters chose this option. To many Scots, a strong Scottish identity thus appears to have been seen to be perfectly compatible with Labour's policies of devolution as much as with SNP policies of independence in Europe.

As Labour came to be the main standard bearer of Scottish nationalism, its goals were naturally redefined. Unlike the SNP, Labour's support for Scottish nationalism never included independence as the solution to Scotland's problems; the goal remained a strong Scotland within a united Britain. The SNP and Labour, however, always agreed on the nature of Scottish nationalism as 'civic' not 'ethnic'. Rather than being preoccupied with classic nationalist concerns for the vitality of culture and heritage, Labour's devolution rhetoric emphasised a more pragmatic focus on what could be done to change Scotland's democratic deficit and, as a result, Scotland's poor socio-economic state of affairs.

The Scottish Constitutional Convention
The Campaign for a Scottish Assembly (CSA) was established in 1980. Its members, representatives from the political sphere (Labour, the Liberals, the SNP and the Communist Party), academics and representatives from the STUC, for the first time sat down in plenary to discuss how best to achieve an increased measure of autonomy for Scotland. The goal of the CSA was to get home rule back on the political agenda, and it was believed that the only way to do this was to bring together all Scottish nationalists and work towards a united claim.

Another significant development, closely related to the CSA, was the publication from the early 1980s of the magazine *Radical Scotland*. This was a forum for debate, mainly by the left and nationalist groupings in Scottish politics. Academics, literati and politicians of established and future prominence contributed to the magazine. All walks of Scottish non-Conservative life had an opportunity to voice their opinions and concerns in a forum where politicians would listen to them directly. The magazine was blatantly anti-Conservative, and pro-home rule. It led the fight against the Poll Tax and, significantly, strongly supported the CSA initiative to create a Constitutional Convention.

In July 1988, after the 1987 General Election had manifested the power of the Conservatives, the CSA produced a report, *A Claim of Right for Scotland*, recommending that a Constitutional Convention including representatives from all political parties and civil society be set up with the purpose of assembling support for constitutional change.[13] Although the Conservatives refused to be part of the scheme, in 1989 the Scottish Constitutional Convention (SCC) sat for the first time. In it, most of civil and political society in Scotland now joined hands to try to bring about some kind of devolution of powers from Westminster. The SCC included Scottish MPs from Labour, the Liberal Democrats, the SNP (who would, however, later abandon the

SCC), and representatives from many other walks of life in Scotland, including the Orkney and Shetland Movement, Scottish MEPs, STUC, the Scottish Churches, and *An Comunn Gaidhealach*.[14]

The SCC published its final document, *Scotland's Parliament. Scotland's Right* on St. Andrew's Day, 30 November 1995. The document, which would become the basis for New Labour's program for devolution, illustrates yet again the emphasis that Scottish political nationalism places on non-ethno-cultural elements, such as socio-economic considerations and democracy:

> The first and greatest reason for creating a Scottish parliament is that the people of Scotland want and deserve democracy. Their will is powerful and clear. This is a democratic deficit which runs contrary to Scotland's distinct political identity and system. It is affecting relations with the rest of the United Kingdom in which most Scots wish to remain, and hampering Scotland's ability to make its voice heard in the world, particularly within a fast-developing European Union well attuned to such voices. Scotland's Parliament will be able to make a real difference to the prosperity of the people of Scotland, and to the quality of life they lead. [T]he Scottish economy can be differentiated from those of other parts of the UK, both in its strengths and in its weaknesses.[15]

Cooperation across social and political boundaries had thus produced a document which showed the remarkable consensus that had been achieved by this time, as well as a previously rarely voiced confidence in Scotland's ability to govern itself. Cooperation, consensus and confidence were the three essentials that would come to characterise Scottish political and civil society in the 1990s and provide the energy to boost another surge forward for Scottish nationalism and its demands for constitutional change.

Consensus and devolution
In the period up to 1979, the *Scotsman* – enthusiastically – and the *Glasgow Herald* – reluctantly – had supported the establishment of a Scottish Assembly, but many Scottish newspapers, particularly those on the right, opposed it. By the mid-1990s, however, the situation was altogether different. Now all Scottish-based newspapers, except for the *Sunday Post* – 'that bastion of conservative values'[16] – and the *Dundee Courier*, opposed the continuation of Conservative government.[17] With the exceptions of the *Dundee Courier* and the *Press and Journal*, all Scottish papers supported a Scottish parliament. In Maurice Smith's words: 'To be pro-Home Rule was to be politically correct'.[18]

Significantly, and in contrast to previous periods of nationalist surges, confidence and cross-disciplinary cooperation would also, in the 1980s and

1990s, characterise the cultural sphere of Scottish society, which would in many ways blaze the trail for institutions such as the Scottish Constitutional Convention. The last two decades of the twentieth century saw a significant degree of confluence between cultural expression and politically and socio-economically motivated nationalist demands. Previously, Scottish cultural nationalism and canonical culture had largely been seen as a refuge or retreat from Scotland's unpleasant political and socio-economic realities. Now some literati were actively trying to change aspects of that reality by becoming involved in the debate, either directly or via the literature they produced. Cairns Craig speaks of the emergence of a new and vigorous debate 'about the nature of Scottish experience [...] and about the ways in which the Scottish situation related to that of other similar cultures throughout the world'.[19] The writers of the cultural sphere thus 'crossed the border' to the political sphere and offered their assistance to political nationalism, and they were not alone in doing so. Popular rock bands and singers such as Runrig, The Proclaimers and Fish were highly critical of what they generally regarded as a malfunctioning established system, and proscribed Scottish pride and political nationalism as the cure for Scotland's ills.

Those in other spheres, politicians, administrators and academics, in turn crossed borders to enter the cultural realm. An important outlet for writers of the cultural revival as well as a forum for debate about Scottish culture and identity was the magazine *Cencrastus*, established like *Radical Scotland* in the wake of the 1979 devolution referendum in an attempt to 'rekindle flames'.[20] Editorials as well as contributions testify to the political overtones always present in the magazine. Political were also the front page illustrations: one of the more famous covers shows a Hugh MacDiarmid-faced rampant Scottish lion clad in the Saltire, its tail an ink-dripping pen, trampling a frayed Union Jack under foot.[21] Sociologists, political scientists, literary critics, writers and filmmakers met in these forums and made the cultural revival more than the rebirth of the cultural sphere of society.

The bonds that now characterised the relationship between political and cultural nationalism in Scotland were certainly closer and stronger than had ever been the case before. The redefinition of Scottish identity and society had become the common ground on which actors from the political, socio-economic and cultural spheres could meet. Perhaps it was because the cultural sphere had not been particularly involved in the political nationalist battles fought in the 1970s that it was sooner to recover from the 1979 setback than the political sphere. The result was a new cultural nationalism of a much more political kind, and where political nationalism in the 1960s arose almost in spite of old tartan-clad romantic notions of cultural nationalism, political nationalism and cultural voices in the 1980s and 1990s met more often in fruitful exchanges. These took many forms, some of them critical and satirical, but most of them also illustrating a renewed sense of pride in many aspects of the Scottish reality.

The 1997 general election, in which the Scots did not return a single Conservative MP, resulted in a landslide victory for Tony Blair's 'New Labour' and, as a direct consequence, a change of central government policy towards constitutional change in the UK. On 11 September 1997, referendums were held in both Wales and Scotland to decide whether there was popular support for the devolution of powers through the establishment of elected assemblies in these parts of the UK. The Scottish Parliament would be able to legislate on a wide range of areas, including health, education, transport, social work, housing, economic development, the legal system, environment, the arts – and would have the powers to regulate taxes by up to 3 pence in the pound (by critics referred to as the 'Tartan Tax').

11 September 1997 saw the Scots vote massively in favour of the reestablishment of the Scottish Parliament. 74.3 per cent of the voters were in favour of devolution, 63.5 per cent voted in favour of giving the parliament tax-varying powers. The Scottish Parliament was re-established and re-convened on 1 July 1999.

Conclusion

A difference in the mood in Scotland in 1979, by the time of the first referendum, and in 1997, by the time of the second referendum, is clearly discernible. On the basis of such a comparison it is tempting to try to discover the 'recipe' for successful Scottish nationalism. However, no single explanation can be given as to what exactly brought about the three essentials of cooperation, consensus and confidence in Scottish society over a little less than two decades, to produce the last irresistible wave of nationalism. Nor is it possible to set up a simple causal chain to show how one essential was the precondition of another. It is possible, however, to outline some of the most influential processes and incentives.

As illustrated above, negative incentives for nationalism did not disappear in the era of Conservative government. On the contrary, the Conservative neo-liberal assault on what were considered Scottish institutions, along with a sense of political impotence resulting from a democratic deficit, served to alienate another large (middle class) segment of Scottish society from Westminster rule and the constitutional status quo. To these negative incentives were, furthermore, added crucial positive ones. Firstly, further European integration promised to act as a safety net that deflated the unionist warnings of economic and social disaster in case of any measure of devolution; secondly, a newly revitalised and voter-appealing Labour Party stood forth as the convinced champion of the devolutionist cause; and thirdly, Scotland's cultural revival spurred new confidence, both by its international successes and by its spilling into and adding to other spheres of public life. Somewhere along the line of events and processes, the positive incentives tipped the balance to help Scottish nationalism overcome the 'cringe'.

Notes

[1] Tom Nairn, *The Break-Up of Britain: Crisis and Neo-Nationalism* (London: New Left Books 1977), p. 156.
[2] BBC News, 28 February 2004, 'I want to end the Scottish cringe' [URL: http://news.bbc.co.uk/1/hi/scotland/3494686.stm].
[3] Christopher Harvie, 'Nationalism, Journalism and Cultural Politics' in Tom Gallagher (ed.), *Nationalism in the Nineties* (Edinburgh: Polygon 1991), pp. 29-45, p. 31.
[4] Jack Brand, *The National Movement in Scotland* (London: Routledge & Kegan Paul 1978), p. 62.
[5] Michael Lynch, *Scotland: A New History*. 2nd ed. (London: Pimlico 1992), p. 446.
[6] Scottish National Party, 'General Election Manifesto, February 1974' (Edinburgh 1974), p. 4; original emphasis.
[7] See e.g. David McCrone, *The Sociology of Nationalism* (London: Routledge 1998), pp. 127-8.
[8] Most notably by Craig Beveridge and Ronald Turnbull in *The Eclipse of Scottish Culture* (Edinburgh: Polygon 1989).
[9] Michael Keating, *Nations against the State: The New Politics of Nationalism in Quebec, Catalonia and Scotland* (Houndmills: Macmillan 1996), p. 176.
[10] David McCrone, *Understanding Scotland: The Sociology of a Stateless Nation* (London: Routledge 1992), p. 173.
[11] Scottish National Party, 'Scotland's Future – Independence in Europe. Manifesto: European Elections' (Edinburgh, 15 June 1989).
[12] Keating p. 175.
[13] Campaign for a Scottish Assembly, *A Claim of Right for Scotland* (Edinburgh, 1988).
[14] Scottish Constitutional Convention, *Scotland's Parliament. Scotland's Right* (Edinburgh 1995), pp. 34-5.
[15] Scottish Constitutional Convention pp. 6-7.
[16] Maurice Smith, *Paper Lions: The Scottish Press and National Identity* (Edinburgh: Polygon 1994), p. 175.
[17] John MacInnes, 'The Press in Scotland', *Scottish Affairs* 1, 1992, pp. 137-149, p. 143.
[18] Smith p. 15.
[19] Cairns Craig, 'Series Preface' in Maurice Smith, *Paper Lions: The Scottish Press and National Identity* (Edinburgh: Polygon 1994), pp. vi-vii.
[20] *Cencrastus*. 'Revaluation', *Cencrastus* 10:3, 1982, p. 3.
[21] *Cencrastus*. Cover. *Cencrastus* 32, 1989.

THE SCOTS LANGUAGE THEN AND NOW

Graham D. Caie

Abstract

Scots was the language of kings and officialdom until the 17th century when power and thence linguistic prestige travelled south. It was also the language of great poets such as Henryson, Dunbar, Lindsay and Douglas. However, by the 18th century it was common in "polite society" to purge one's writings and speech of "Scotticisms" and school children were strongly encouraged to avoid such "substandard slang", as Scots was associated with the working classes and rural communities. Scots is now enjoying a renaissance, started by the Lallans movement, and there are many current movements to promote the language, in spite of problems surrounding attempts to create a standard written variety of Scots.

This is an exciting period for those interested in the Scots language. There is a new Cultural Policy for Scotland which backs the promotion of Scots through the Scottish Language Dictionary project and the concept of an Institute for the Languages of Scotland. The Scottish Parliament has set up a cross-party group to look into the question of upholding and promoting Scots and there are many other organisations such as the Scots Language Resource Centre, the Scots Language Society and projects such as the Scots Corpus at Glasgow University which are doing much to promote the language. Students can learn Scots at some schools and universities and the earlier stigma attached to the language is slowly disappearing.

What is Scots?
I will call Scots a language (or 'leid' in Scots), as it is acknowledged as a minority language by the EU (European Charter for Regional or Minority Languages). The difference between language and dialect is much disputed, but it is generally considered a socio-political rather than a linguistic construct. The differences in lexis, syntax and pronunciation make Scots as distinct from English as Swedish is from Danish and there is the same population in Scotland and Denmark. Scots is also spoken in Northern Ireland where it is called Ulster Scots. Scots covers a very broad continuum, from what might be called 'dense' or 'braid' Scots (e.g., 'Fou ar ye dein?'; How are you? or 'Fit fit fits fit?'; Which foot fits which? in the north-east

Doric dialect) to Scottish Standard English (SSE) which has only a few features of Scots (e.g., the use of 'wee' for small, or 'aye' for 'yes'). SSE is the variety normally used in formal, non-fictional written texts in Scotland and in spoken form would have differences in pronunciation (e.g., the rhotic <r>), lexis and syntax. It can be heard on TV and radio. The majority of the five million Scots would admit to speaking SSE, whereas it is estimated that 1.7 million speak the denser variety.

The term Lallans is sometimes given to Scots; however, this refers to the Lowland dialect in its written form and was applied by Hugh MacDiarmid, Douglas Young and their circle at the time of the Scottish Renaissance (beginning of the 20th century) to the variety of synthetic Scots which is a blend of different dialects and both contemporary and archaic forms. Their idea was to create a standard written Scots which would be used in a variety of genres, in particular literature. The Lallans movement continues today with its own journal of that name.

In contrast there are about 58,000 Gaelic speakers in Scotland, many of whom live in the western isles or the Highlands. The Gaelic Language Act of 2005 gave the language stronger official recognition and many road signs in the Highlands and parliamentary documents are now translated into Gaelic. There is among some Scots language promoters a slight irritation that the Gaelic movement with fewer speakers is given more funding, has television programmes and is more accepted as a language of Scotland than Scots. The majority of Scots speakers, however, see a common cause in promoting the languages of Scotland. It is much easier for Gaelic speakers to demonstrate that they speak a different language than it is for Scots speakers and it was significant that the General Register Office refused to include the question 'Do you speak Scots?' in the 2001 census, as they thought that many would not be certain how to respond. Greater linguistic awareness is needed of what Scots is and isn't.

As can be inferred from the above, Scots is alive and well as a spoken language, albeit in many different regional varieties. It is also thriving amongst creative writers in Scotland and Ulster, although every author has to devise his or her own written variety which reflects their own Scots dialect. Lallans aimed at making one variety, albeit artificial, as a standard written for all; it could then be used in mass media and in official documents, such as those produced by the Scottish Parliament and, very important, in schools. There has, however, been a strong backlash against any attempt to have a standard written variety for a number of reasons: i) as all Scots can read standard English it is not necessary to create a new variety; ii) Scots could never agree on any one system, especially if it privileged one dialect; iii) many object that it would create chaos if all school children had to learn a different spelling systems (e.g., to write 'scuil' as well as 'school'); iv) authors want to convey the sounds and vocabulary of their own dialect, not a synthetic one; v) foreigners would find this language difficult to read and this would have consequences for the tourist trade; and vi) Scots over the years has been associated with lower class, urban communities, and so would be socially disadvantageous for anyone with ambitions of upward social mobility.

Scots for many people even today is seen as sub-standard, the language of comedy, the music hall and the pub; for generations (though not today) it was banned from the school-room as sub-standard, inferior or at best colloquial. It is, however, resurrected at times such as Burns Night when whisky brings out 'scotticisms' such as 'wee', 'couthy' or 'bonnie'; then it is wrapped up in cotton wool for the next occasion. Such an attitude is often called 'the tartanisation of Scots' and reflects Scots' love-hate relationship with their language: it is like a comfortable pair of slippers that you love to relax in, but would not wear in public. The reasons for this negative or at best ambiguous attitude to Scots can be found in the history of the language.

The History of Scots
So where does Scots come from? Lowland Scots comes basically from a dialect of Anglo-Saxon, Old Northumbrian, which contained many Norse elements, as one might expect from its north-eastern location. It was found in south-eastern Scotland up to the Firth of Forth from the 7th century onwards, while the rest of the country was speaking varieties of Celtic. Up to the first half of the 11th century most of Scotland, including the king, Malcolm III (called Canmore; died 1093), spoke a Celtic language. Although the Norman Conquest in 1066 did not include Scotland, Malcolm gave refuge to many Anglo-Saxon royals and nobles and married the English Princess Margaret; when Northumbria was harshly tamed by William, many Northumbrian-speaking refugees came to Scotland, and so Inglis, as it was called, was spoken in the south-east of Scotland. The burghs in particularly were English speaking and so the language spread and developed in Lowland Scotland, the east coast in particular. By the 14th century, Scots was developing separately from north-east English, and fast becoming a prestige language spoken by all from the king downwards. The need for national identity in the 14th and 15th centuries also played an important part, as there is nothing more important than a national language to create a separate identity. Such an argument is made today, especially by those who embrace independence for Scotland.

It was not until 1375, however, that we find our first major literary work in Scots, Barbour's *Brus*, an epic poem celebrating King Robert's exploits in the War of Independence and the Battle of Bannockburn (1314) in particular. King James I of Scotland wrote a love allegory, *The Kingis Quair*, in Scots, dedicated to his English wife, Joan Beaufort, in the early 15th century and this was followed by the impressive flowering of Scottish literature by the poets William Dunbar, Gavin Douglas, Robert Henryson and David Lindsay. C. S. Lewis called the 15th century 'the drab age' of English poetry, but this cannot be said of Scottish literature which enjoyed a major renaissance.

Scots at this time grew confident in their language which had a number of registers, thanks to the blending of French (from the Auld Alliance, Mary Queen of Scots, etc.), and Dutch (from trading links) with native Celtic, Anglo-Saxon and Norse vocabulary. Examples are:

a) from Dutch (Flemish): golf, loun (rascal), kyte (belly), scone (*schoonbroot*), pinkie (little finger), skink (shin of ham) and dubs (mud).

b) from French: dams (draughts), ashet (plate), aumrie (cupboard), douce (sweet), pouch (pocket) and the less elegant, gardyloo ('gardez l'eau' or 'watch out!'), to cowp (topple), to fash oneself (to get angry or disturbed).

c) from Norse: lug (ear), tike (dog), kist (chest), flit (move house), dyke (stone wall), brig (bridge), to laup (leap), to big (build) and biggings (building) and gate (road), brae (hill), brambles (blackberries).

d) from Old English: to dree (suffer), byre (barn), handsel (gift), eneuch (enough), ilka (each), leid (language), unco (unknown, very), syne (since)

Dunbar, for example, was a poet who could adopt either the Scots of Edinburgh streets, as in *The Flyting of Dunbar and Kennedy*, in which the vocabulary is largely 'native', that is of Old English or Old Norse derivation:

> Than rynis thow doun the gait with gild of boyis,   [street]
> And all the toun tykis hingand in thy heilis;   [dogs]
> Of laidis and lownis thair rysis sic ane noyis [...].   [lads]
> Fische wyvis cryis fy, and castis doun skillis and skeilis   [baskets and pails]

Or aureate diction, based on French and Latin vocabulary, in *The Golden Targe*:

Full angellike thir birdis sang their houris
Within thair courtyns grene, in to thair bouris
Apparalit quhite and rede wyth blomes suete;
Anamalit was the felde wyth all colouris,
The perly droppis schake in silvir schouris.

The 15th and 16th centuries saw the highest point of the Scots language. It was spoken in all regional areas, except the Gaelic west and north, and by all social groups. All authors in both England and Scotland in the period up to the invention of printing wrote as well as spoke their own dialectal varieties, but this changed when printing led to the need to 'fix' the language and find a variety which all could read. The age of written dialects was then over in England, largely for economic reasons, and so gradually a standard written form emerged, much as it is today. This explains the complexity of modern English with spellings such as 'night' and 'bough' and 'laugh' with the <gh>, all of which had a [x] sound up to this time. Then, as England was ahead of Scotland in printing, the English written variety was also adopted in Scotland, as it would be too expensive to have books printed in different varieties of English.

The Decline
The decline of Scots began in the 16th century, before the Union of the Crowns and parliaments. The Reformation saw the adoption of the Geneva Bible and an English Psalter in Scotland, and so the new Protestant religion read the Word of God in English and along with the English Bible came all the theological and philosophical writings in this age of expansion in literacy. God and all learning were considered English and this was intensified with the appearance of the King James Bible. It is interesting to note that it was not until the 20th century that a Bible in Scots appeared, translated by Lorimer, but it is rarely used in churches today, and when it is many are embarrassed to hear the Word of God in a language they consider too colloquial. The Catholic backlash at the Reformation used this as a weapon and accused the reformers of treacherous abandonment of their native language by writing *suddrone*, 'southern'. To be fair to the reformers, they were more interested in the spread of the new word than in the medium by which it was spread, and, as there existed English translations of the major texts, they did not spend time making a new translation into Scots. Inadvertently, they did their language a great disservice.

The Union of the Crowns in 1603 and the Treaty of Union in 1707 focussed power and all political attention on London. Those who went south with the king quickly adapted to 'English English' after being ridiculed and misunderstood. Many who could afford it sent their sons to be educated in England, including John Knox. Gradually, Scots declined in its prestige and Edinburgh saw an influx of elocution teachers who were willing to purge Scots of all his or her 'scotticisms'. One teacher advertised as a selling point the fact that he will not allow any 'Scotch' to be spoken in his classes. Allan Ramsay in 1754 founded the Select Society, later The Society for the English Language, whose aim was 'to teach the pronunciation of the English tongue with propriety and grace', thence to aid social advancement. David Hume, the philosopher, had his writings vetted for infelicitous Scottish words or expressions. Lists were made of Scotticisms to be avoided, such as 'a sore head' for 'headache'; 'go to my bed' for 'go to bed'; 'he has got the cold' for 'got a cold'; 'a bit bread' for 'a bit of bread'; 'stay' for 'live'. Teachers were also encouraged to purge all Scots from their pupils, as it was considered 'degenerate', 'vulgar' and 'slipshod'. Such an attitude continued until the mid-20th century when more enlightened school inspectors could see the value in what they now call 'the language the children bring to school.'

Today
All Scots speakers are diglossial, that is, they can shift from the 'prestigious' dialect of English to the vernacular regional dialect, depending on the circumstances. So the language of the playground may well be very different from the school-room, that of the pulpits from that of the pub.

Today the situation is much more relaxed and teachers are encouraging students to express themselves in Scots, if they wish. One teacher, John Hodgart, writes:

> If we cannae learn how tae cope wi educatin oor weans in their native languages, saw that Scots an English complement ane anither, oor educational system will continue tae fail Scottish culture as it hae duin owre language.
>
> (*The Scots Language: Its Place in Education*, eds. Liz Niven and Robin Jackson. Dundee, 1998, p. 3.)

The debate continues whether there will ever be a national standard written variety and many look to Norway with its two official variants. Reports from the Scottish Parliament do sometimes appear in Scots, such as:

Education, Culture an Sport Comatee, 2nt Report 2003
The feck o submissions in writin concentratit on the Scots leid. While mony submissions focused on Scots an the education system, it is clear that the weys

that language is treatit inwith education an inwith culture is inextricably thirled. A want o awnin Scots in schuils will lead tae bruckleness for the leid. Screivers o the future will tyne the ability tae communicate in Scots. Gin cultural resources in Scots isnae produced ony mair for an by theatre, television, literature or poetry, syne reference will be tint an there will be derth o teachin maitter.

However, there are still many prejudices against Scots which is considered by many as less prestigious than English, working class and simply 'bad English'. Although about 1.5 million of the 5 million Scots in the country speak Scots, the majority of these will not normally acknowledge that they are speaking Scots. One example is a woman who admitted in a broad Scots dialect that she spoke Scots when living in 'the scheme' (housing estate) but that now when in better accommodation she claims she doesn't, thereby equating social conditions with language.

What is the answer to this common prejudice which hinders the spread and acceptance of Scots? One solution is through education: by teaching the history of Scots, that is, the etymology of lexical terms, the sources of syntactic structures and pronunciation, we can begin to show that the language has a strong pedigree and is not a colloquial, slovenly 'gutter' patio, as it has at times been called. The rise, fall and gradual renaissance of Scots reflects the social, economic and political history of Scotland.

Bibliography:

Corbett, John; Derrick McClure; Jane Stuart-Smith (eds) (2003) *The Edinburgh Companion to Scots*. Edinburgh, Edinburgh University Press.
Eagle, Andy (2005) *Wir Ain Leid*. Scots-Online. Available at http://www.scots-online.org/airticles/WirAinLeid.pdf.
Dictionary of the Scots Language. http://www.dsl.ac.uk/dsl/
Jones, Charles (1997) *The Edinburgh History of the Scots Language*. Edinburgh, University of Edinburgh Press.
Kay, Billy (1993) *The Mither Tongue*. Alloway Publishing.
MacAfee, Caroline (1980/1992) 'Characteristics of Non-Standard Grammar in Scotland' (University of Aberdeen: available at http://www.abdn.ac.uk/~enl038/grammar.htm)
McLeod, D (1997) *Why Scots Matters.*, Edinburgh.
Murison, D (1977) *The Guid Scots Tongue.*, Edinburgh.
Niven, Liz; Robin Jackson (Eds.) (1998) *The Scots Language: its place in education*. Watergaw Publications.
Scottish National Dictionary Association (1999) *Concise Scots Dictionary* .

Edinburgh, Polygon.
Scottish Language Dictionaries at www.scotsdictionaries.org.uk/
Warrack, Alexander (Editor)(1911) *Chambers Scots Dictionary*. Chambers.

THAT DEAR GREEN PLACE REWRITTEN: ALASDAIR GRAY AND SCOTTISH LITERARY INDEPENDENCE

Karina Westermann

Abstract

Since his 1981 debut, *Lanark*, Alasdair Gray has been a central figure in Scottish arts and literature. This paper examines Gray's creative output and traces his influence upon generations of Scottish writers. Issues such as devolution, the use of Scots in contemporary Scottish literature and the sense of Scottish identity are addressed throughout the paper, using Gray's oeuvre as a point of reference.

In 2006 Glasgow's popular Kelvingrove art gallery and museum reopened after a lengthy refurbishment. A focal point in Glasgow's West End, the museum's red sandstone spires stretch towards the sky with an enthusiasm that only the extravagant Victorian industrialists could muster. The sprawling building with its faux Gothic ornamentation is what remains of the huge exhibition hall built for the Great Exhibition in 1901; it lies uneasily across from a sports hall and a modern hospital. Its awkward position does not dilute the absurdities of the building, but Kelvingrove is served well by being juxtaposed with run-down modernity. Inside the museum its curators have taken inspiration from the idea of juxtaposition: a Spitfire can be found amongst a flock of birds in an exploration of the idea of flight; a *papier-mâché* statue of Elvis Presley is within walking distance of Dali's *The Christ of St. John of the Cross*. Perhaps the greatest juxtaposition of all is the sheer magnitude of the building itself against the pragmatic approach of the museum.

One of Kelvingrove's most interesting features is how the notion of Scottish identity runs through the museum. Britain's imperial past is addressed head-on with hard questions asked about Scotland's involvement in slavery and the slaughter of natives in faraway wars. The Holocaust is examined with stories told by Glaswegian survivors. The section on British wildlife even features the notoriously shy haggis animal (which bears an astonishing resemblance to a badger with extra bits of wild fur glued to its head). Other displays explore Glasgow's multiculturalism and also the historical background to the continuing presence of sectarianism within the city (as exemplified by its rival football clubs, Glasgow Rangers and Celtic). While the sense of Scotland (and particularly the Glaswegian sense of Scotland) runs through the entire museum, Kelvingrove's curators have devoted a small section to a direct questioning of what constitutes Scottish identity.

Scotland carries many myths and legends: the massacre at Glen Coe; the brave Mary Queen of Scots; the dignified failure of Bonnie Prince Charlie; the brutal Highland clearances. The public imagination has been caught by its violent past as romanticized in popular Hollywood treatments such as *Braveheart* and *Rob Roy*. BBC productions such as the long-running *Monarch of the Glen* series have served to reinforce an image of traditional countryside values and quaint Scottish folk. Tourist shops continue to flog tartan, bagpipe music, reproduction claymores and bad paintings of noble Highland stags. Kelvingrove encompasses all these stories and more. However, it also asks whether these portrayals and myths are at all emblematic of contemporary Scotland or whether they form part of an idealized past constructed to keep Scotland tied to a colonial identity: Robert Burns is humorously recast as a late 18th century Che Guevara using his native language to poetic revolutionary effect; wearing tartan becomes detached from its historical context and is reterritorialised by English fashionistas (both 19th and 21st century) and the majestic Scottish landscape is subverted by a photo montage of a stylized contemporary Scottish living room filled with local brands and popular entertainment. A subversive and darkly humorous take on Scotland and the identity of her people is thus juxtaposed with the idealised tourist version.

Kelvingrove serves as a good example of how Scottish identity is being perceived, re-constructed and communicated by creative local people. In a celebrated piece of art entitled 'The Kelvingrove Eight' by Calum Colvin on display in Edinburgh's National Portrait Gallery of Scotland, eight artists and writers are seen gathered in a living room overlooking Kelvingrove. It is a stylised piece but it refers to a group of people meeting during the early 1970s in Glasgow's West End - only a short walk away from Kelvingrove itself.

In the apartment of Philip Hobsbaum, literary critic, Glasgow-based writers, playwrights and artists were introduced to each other's works and even if they initially did not have much in common, a sense of creative community and identity was to grow from these gatherings. In the postscript to the 1985 short story collection *Lean Tales*, the writer and artist Alasdair Gray invokes these informal literary evenings, hinting that geographical proximity gave rise to creative proximity.[1] When Gray took up mentoring Glasgow University's creative writing workshop in the early 2000s, he did so alongside novelist James Kelman and poet Tom Leonard - two writers who had also been members of Hobsbaum's 1970s literary evenings. Gray again brings up Hobsbaum's contribution to making Glasgow a meeting place for emerging writers in his preface to *The Knuckle End*, a 2004 anthology of 'the best new writing in Scotland' partly based upon Gray and Kelman's writing course.[2]

Although his name may be less well-known outside Scotland than either the Booker Prize-winning James Kelman or the widely anthologised Tom Leonard, Alasdair Gray's position within the Scottish literary canon is firmly established. His first novel, the epic *Lanark – A Life in Four Books*,[3] was hailed as an instant classic upon its publication in 1981. Though a notoriously difficult novel to summarise with its ever shifting layers of storytelling, it is at its core a *Bildungsroman*: the story of Duncan Thaw, a young Glasgow artist and his apparent suicide which turns him into the eponymous Lanark, who arrives in the city of Unthank in search of redemption but ends up (maybe) destroying himself along the way. Its structure is wilfully strange: the book begins *in medias res* with Lanark arriving in Unthank; continues with Thaw's very Scottish childhood before following Thaw's perceived failure at life and returning to Lanark's battle with the author of the book.

One of the most quoted passages of *Lanark* deals directly with the question of imagining Scotland, and particularly Glasgow, into existence:

> 'Glasgow is a magnificent city,' said McAlpin. 'Why do we hardly ever notice that?'
> 'Because nobody imagines living there,' said Thaw. [...] '[Think] of Florence, Paris, London, New York. Nobody visiting them for the first time is a stranger because he's already visited them in paintings, novels, history books and films. But if a city hasn't been used by an artist not even the inhabitants live there imaginatively.' (243)

Alasdair Gray places Glasgow on the map by actively re-imagining it as a place of contrasts, juxtapositions, and endless possibilities. His Duncan Thaw inhabits a recognisable Glasgow with all its landmarks: Kelvingrove Park, the Glasgow School of Art, the bizarre Necropolis (a vast burial ground for Victorian merchants which overlooks central Glasgow) and the bourgeois West End. The realist semi-autobiographical narrative is juxtaposed with the fantastical, outlandish Unthank where daylight is but a distant memory, people slowly turn into dragons and mouths grow like tumours on people's bodies. Yet despite the surrealism, the Kafkaesque Unthank remains a recognisable Glasgow. Gray is doing exactly what his protagonist was asking for: he is using his city imaginatively.

There have been other Glasgow novels – most notably McArthur and

Long's *No Mean City* from 1935 and Hind's *The Dear Green Place* from 1966 – but, as Beat Wischi puts it, 'The real problem of Glasgow writing was not "how to write about *Glasgow*" but rather "*how* to write about Glasgow" (68).[4] Most Glasgow novels had been grim, realist depictions of hard working-class life and poor people down on their luck. *Lanark* showed that a Glasgow novel could be different. The novel is no less grim than its predecessors – but Gray finds flashes of redemption within the darkness: The streets are dirty, the city is poor but you have the powers of imagination and the human spirit on your side. Not only can hope be found in displacement (whether geographical or psychological), but a sense of identity can also be found through rejecting established notions of what it means to be a white, male Briton.

Lanark can be read as an example of postcolonial literature rebelling against the traditional (English) realist novel. Instead of taking his cue from the Dickensian school of realist urban writing, Gray looks towards Scottish literature. Robin Jenkins' *The Cone-Gatherers* from 1955 is a case in point. It is a realist novel set in the countryside during World War II. Two brothers arrive at a country estate to gather cones in order to replant trees. Their arrival causes strife between the classes and the brothers end up having to fight for their lives. However, there is a rich symbolic undercurrent to *The Cone-Gatherers*: the book is ultimately about Scotland's ability to rebuild itself despite class differences and religious fanaticism. While the symbolism is heavy-handed, Jenkins' identification of Otherness as a Scottish trait anticipates *Lanark* as does the use of several shifting narrative levels. Other Scottish writers who have clearly served as sources of inspiration include James Hogg and Robert Louis Stevenson, with their use of the *Doppelgänger* motif and the idea of everyday, soulless evil.

Lanark was published only a few years after the referendum of 1979 wherein a proposed independent Scottish parliament was rejected. Despite the book being several decades in the making – Gray began writing it as a semi-autobiographical novel in the late 1950s and developed its fantastical elements along the way – it has been viewed as capturing the *Zeitgeist* and as making a strong case for a particular sense of Scottishness. These words from Angus Calder may be representative of the praise heaped upon the novel:

> The publication of Alasdair Gray's novel *Lanark* in 1981 seemed even at the time to mark an epoch. On the face of it, the book was pessimistic, ending in the apocalyptic destruction of Glasgow. But the scale of its conception and the wit of its execution were both inspirational.[5]

Several younger writers have been heavily inspired by *Lanark*. Iain Banks is a prolific Fife-based author of both so-called 'literary' fiction and speculative fiction (the latter under the name of Iain M. Banks). Banks has in interviews cheerfully acknowledged his debt to Alasdair Gray's novel:

> *Lanark* absolutely stunned me. I read *Lanark* and I just thought, *Wow!* This is what you can do. It really opened my eyes as to what was possible in fiction. I was just amazed by it. My own novel, *The Bridge*, I don't think would have been anything like it turned out if it had not been for *Lanark*.[6]

The Bridge (1986) may carry its inspiration like a badge – even its table of contents owes a great deal to Alasdair Gray's trademark typographical trickery – but it inhabits a sinister imaginative world of its own. A man, John Orr, lies in a coma after a traffic accident on the Firth of Forth Bridge connecting Fife with Leith. In his coma, Orr also inhabits the world of The Bridge – a dark world of thresholds, voids, shadows; a world where orthography breaks down and characters have to redefine/rediscover themselves before they can break away. Hal Duncan's piece of urban speculative fiction, *Vellum: The Book of All Hours* (2005) goes even further than Gray. While *Lanark*'s Glasgow was turned into the hellish Unthank, Duncan argues that Glasgow has the capacity to encompass the entire world within it. Using multiple narrative levels, he reimagines Glasgow's West End captured within a book as the gateway to an even greater world both familiar and unfamiliar. James Robertson's *The Fanatic* (1999) is a reworking of traditional historical fiction using the familiar Scottish trope of *Doppelgänger* whilst dissolving time and space. It is less radical than either Banks or Duncan, but Robertson's mentally ill protagonist reads like a modern Duncan Thaw losing his sense of identity within an Edinburgh oddly evocative of Gray's Glasgow. In a sense, this has perhaps been *Lanark*'s greatest achievement: the book has successfully challenged Edinburgh's status as Scotland's city of literature.

Alasdair Gray has never quite succeeded in replicating *Lanark*'s success, but he has maintained a steady following throughout the ensuing decades. His next novel, the dark and erotic *1982 Janine*, was easy to admire for its technical scope but more difficult to love. The book famously features a nervous breakdown, one which is neither told nor described in a particularly 'normal' or literary manner. As the protagonist Jock McLeish breaks down, the text offers a similar semantic breakdown, which is also reflected in the layout. It splits into a 'ministry of voices' – a cacophonous choir of voices inside Jock McLeish's head depicted by several typographies competing for dominance in front of the reader's eyes. As the reading eye attempts to capture all the printed voices simultaneously, it experiences a 'reading' breakdown similar to the breakdown represented on and by the printed page.

1982 Janine's story of a failed small-time Scotsman can easily be lost to readers distracted by the formal virtuosity. Gray's intense exploration of power and powerlessness (both political and sexual) can likewise also seem overshadowed by frank (if at their core allegorical) depictions of sexual fantasies. It is perhaps his most overtly political novel. *1982 Janine* sees Alasdair Gray addressing the 1979 referendum through the eyes of a whisky-drinking downtrodden middle-aged man:

> The truth is that we are a nation of arselickers, though we disguise it with surfaces: a surface of generous, openhanded manliness, a surface of dour practical integrity, a surface of futile maudlin [...] which is why, when England allowed us a referendum on the subject, I voted for Scottish self-government. Not for one minute did I think it would make us more prosperous, we are a poor little country, always have been, always will be, but it would be a luxury to blame ourselves for the mess we are in instead of the bloody old Westminster parliament.[7]

Jock McLeish resentfully lashes out against everyone – including Robert Burns ('Who spread the story that the Scots are an INDEPENDENT people? Robert Burns.' (55)) and the British government for exploiting Scotland's natural resources – and ends up casting himself as a symbol of all Scotland's failures. Scotland has gone from being the land of William Wallace and Robert the Bruce to the land of Jock McLeish, a drunk man looking at a thistle. The self-loathing is palpable but it is a self-loathing propelled by a failure to re-imagine Scotland and being forced to look at his own country through the eyes of a colonised subject. As Will Self notes in his introduction to the Canongate Classics edition of the novel, *1982 Janine* is indeed very much about '1982 Scotland'.

Gray's subsequent publications were easier to digest than *1982 Janine*, but no less political. *The Fall of Kelvin Walker – A Fable of the Sixties* (1985) is an adaptation of an early Gray play. It is a deceptively light-hearted comedic romp in which a self-important Scottish country bumpkin goes to London to pursue a career and girls (although not necessarily in that order). Somehow he manages to insinuate himself into the BBC and becomes a popular, if inefficient television host before losing both his job and his bored English girlfriend. Kelvin has to return to Scotland (possibly for a career in the clergy – a seemingly natural progression from television). The novel's epigraph attributed to JM Barrie is slyly ironic – 'My lady, there are few more impressive sights in the world than a Scotsman on the make' – and yet Kelvin Walker is anything but impressive. He makes his way in the world by parodying his nationality, but as soon as he demands to be taken seriously, he loses whatever influence he may have had.

1990's *Something Leather* is a parenthetical entry in Alasdair Gray's oeuvre. It is a sort of (female) companion piece to *1982 Janine* but lacks its predecessor's narrative punch and formal virtuosity. It revisits familiar territory with sexual encounters exploring notions of power/powerlessness, but its lack of strong story or intriguing characters reduces *Something Leather* to clumsy quasi-pornography. There are redeeming aspects to the book, though: quite apart from being one of Gray's most aesthetically pleasing books – he designs and illustrates his own books[8] – it makes Alasdair Gray's stance on British culture politics abundantly clear.

Glasgow was named European City of Culture in 1990 which meant the city saw an influx of European Union money and artists eager to get a share of the attention awarded to a Glasgow which had seen creative regeneration over the previous ten years or so. While one might have expected the author of *Lanark* to embrace his hometown being recognised as a creative centre, Alasdair Gray's pro-devolution stance caused him promptly to reject the recognition as being too commercial and exploitative. Here we see an English woman, Linda, explaining the events to an English art dealer in a chapter entitled 'Culture Capitalism':

> So Glasgow, which the Lay-ba Party has ruled fo ova half a century, was given the job by the Tory arts minister who announced that Glasgow had set an example of independent action which should be followed by every local authority in the United Kingdom. Wia funding the entaprize out of the rates and public propaty sales and sposaship from banks, oil companies, building societies and whateva we can screw out of Europe.
>
> And Glasgow deserves the job! It's the headquartas of Scottish Opera, Scottish Ballet, Scottish National Orchestra, the Burrell Collection, the Citizen's Theata, the Third Eye Centa and an intanational drama festival: all of them direct and mostly administaed by the English, of course. Sometimes the natives get a bit bolshie about that but I'm very firm with them. I say very quietly, 'Listen! You Scots have been expoating yaw own people to England and everywha else fo centuries, and nobody has complained much about you! Why start howling just because wia giving you a taste of yaw own medicine?' They can't think of an ansa to that one.[9]

There is a real sense of indignation here: Glasgow (and thus Scotland) had enjoyed a surge in creativity among its local writers and artists, but its achievements were being appropriated by what Gray perceives as a colonising power. More to the point, Scottish literature and arts were only appreciated and promoted as long as they could easily be sold to and digested by middle-class England. We return to Linda again:

> Some novels by Glasgow writas had rave reviews in *Times Lit. Sup.*, but I'm afraid they leave me cold. Half seem to have been written in phonetic Scotch about people with names like *Auld Shug*. Every second word seems to be fuck, though hardly any fucking happens. The otha half have complicated plots like SM obstacle races in which I entie-aly lose my way and give up. (174)

These Glasgow writers can easily be identified as Alasdair Gray himself and his old friend from Philip Hobsbaum's writing circle, James Kelman. Gray's satirical comment, '[E]very second word seems to be fuck, though hardly any fucking happens' is oddly prophetic. When James Kelman won the Booker Prize in 1994 for his *How Late It Was, How Late*, his novel was attacked by one of the judges on the board for containing nothing but swearwords. *The Times* was even more hostile and said the judges were glorifying a noble savage.[10] Using demotic Glaswegian Kelman excels in writing harshly realist novels in which he lends voice to people not often credited with having any voice. Compared to Gray's characters who are mostly articulate lower middle-class people, Kelman writes about socially deprived characters who have no language with which to express themselves or enable them to understand their futile lives. Kelman's writerly ability can be misunderstood by readers perplexed by the language he employs, the characters he draws and the situations he captures.

Another aspect of *Something Leather* can be connected to James Kelman. In the 'Acknowledgements' section of *Something Leather*, Alasdair Gray credits the idea of subverting standard English orthography to an unpublished Kelman short story. Raymond Chapman notes:

> If regular spelling is conventionally taken to represent 'normal' speech, understood as the speech of Received Pronunciation without any strong prosodic or phonational features, irregular spelling can render unusual speech, including dialect, substandard or idiophonic pronunciation.[11]

Alasdair Gray subverts this orthographic convention in *Something Leather* by using irregular spelling for Received Pronunciation (R.P.). By doing so, he highlights the implicit hierarchy found in English: the only *right* form of English is the Queen's English[12] with all other dialects of English automatically assumed to be sub-standard. In a novel dealing with issues of power and powerlessness, language is being employed to highlight the struggle between the powerful and the marginalized: Scots is the authoritative standard language in *Something Leather* with R.P. being dismissed as a dialect. The novel sees its author taking charge and claiming ownership of his language. In Scotland, Gray is saying, the language is Scots and everything else is dialect to his ears and eyes. One might argue that Gray actually does very little with his caricature of R.P. but this frustration can be levelled at most aspects of *Something Leather* – an incoherent novel with a hurried, unfinished air.

Linda's complaint that '[half of the novels] seem to have been written in phonetic Scotch' is a common one among certain non-Scottish readers of post-1980 Scottish literature. While James Kelman is the most critically acclaimed, Edinburgh-based Irvine Welsh is probably the most widely read author of the writers reclaiming Scots as a literary language. His debut *Trainspotting* (1993) bled into the mainstream and was turned into a hugely successful film in 1996. Welsh draws upon earlier writers like Kelman and the overlooked Scottish Beat writer Alexander Trocchi (whose Camus-in-Glasgow *Young Adam* (1954) was adapted for the screen in 2003 with some of *Trainspotting*'s actors), but his dark wit and fascination with pop culture struck a nerve with the public that his predecessors never did, nor ever courted. The prolific and versatile Iain Banks uses demotic language to great effect in his novels – both his straight 'literary' ones such as the comedic, if slightly wistful, family mystery *The Crow Road* (1992) and his speculative fiction such as *Feersum Endjinn* (1994). Alan Warner and Anne Donovan are two other contemporary writers opting for the vernacular voice. Warner's *Morvern Callar* (1995) and *The Sopranos* (1998) are both set on Scotland's West Coast and seem determined to provide a snapshot of an eccentric, parochial Scotland distinctly different from the urbanity of Gray's Glasgow and Welsh's Edinburgh. Anne Donovan's affecting and funny *Buddha-Da* (2003) is set in Glasgow's West End, however, and employs three different Glaswegian voices to tell the story of what happens to a family when one of its members suddenly find religion. Incidentally, Donovan was one of the writers to emerge from the tutelage of Alasdair Gray and James Kelman. Admittedly, Scots has been a literary language for centuries – William Dunbar, Robert Burns, and Hugh MacDiarmid spring to mind here – but the recent generations of Scottish writers have used demotic language in an unapologetically celebratory way – encouraging in those who speak the language a growing sense of self and sense of identity.

Having recycled old material in *The Fall of Kelvin Walker* and the rather abysmal *Something Leather*, Alasdair Gray's descent into self-inscribed obscurity was stopped by his 1992 novel, *Poor Things*. It is a playful, mock-Gothic horror story set in Victorian Glasgow. While being Gray's most accessible and instantly likable novel, it is also rather atypical. It features a strong, central and fully rounded female character; it takes place in the past among the upper middle class; the prose style is lively; and the main source of inspiration for the novel is easily discernible as Mary Shelley's *Frankenstein*. After *Poor Things*, which became a moderate success, Alasdair Gray had three more fictional works published before finally securing the financial means necessary to publish his long-term non-fiction project *The Book of Prefaces* (2000).

In preparation since the 1980s, *The Book of Prefaces* is a pleasantly labyrinthine book: it is a collection of prefaces from famous English-language writers. These prefaces are accompanied by (occasionally reliable) glosses and have their own prefaces which in turn have prefaces. Gray's underlying idea behind *The Book of Prefaces* is not only to give a snapshot of English-language literature, but also to emphasise how many of the now canonical writers were tied to a particular sense of place, time and (crucially) community. Great works of art and literature are not lofty, noble or commercial enterprises: they stem from and reflect the lives of ordinary people. Again Gray identifies language as a crucial site of struggle:

> Snobs have always found it easy to pretend that the king or queen's English is theirs, that poorer people cannot think deeply or talk with authority because their homely speech ties them to *common* objects or feelings. England's best writing proves that false. 'Dust to dust and ashes to ashes,' spoken over a grave, means more than 'the transience of human existence.'[13]

and

> At the end of the eighteenth century Robert Burns became the greatest living poet in English, mainly because he used strong forms of speech common among lowland Scots. In south Britain poetry was blighted by a genteel assumption that common speech-forms, like common people, were not truly civilised. (423)

The idea of a community is central to the production of *The Book of Prefaces* itself. It is a joint effort with many prominent Scottish men and women of letters contributing to the glosses – Janice Galloway, James Kelman, A.L. Kennedy, Tom Leonard, Liz Lochhead and Alan Spence among others.[14] Alasdair Gray's selection of texts underlines the communal agenda. Prominence is given to early vernacular versions of the Bible, writers remarking upon Cromwell's Commonwealth, radical political voices of the Enlightenment and 19th century social commentators: all texts engaged with common man and his society. Gray also shows a predilection for writers writing on the outskirts of society: early female novelists and thinkers are included, for instance, as are oddball poets like John Clare and James Thomson. In the postscript to his prefaces, Gray notes he would have included 'those who now write Australian, Asian, African and Caribbean kinds of English' (630): his view of English-language literary history is an inclusive one which actively seeks out the fringes: that is where creativity burns brightest.

Only a few months after Kelvingrove reopened its doors in the corner of Kelvingrove Park, a new Alasdair Gray play opened in Glasgow's West End. *Goodbye Jimmy* (2006) was a short one-hour play put on at the Óran Mór arts venue (which sports one of Scotland's largest pieces of public art – a mural by Gray himself). The play sees God (a Scotsman, of course) arguing with his son (now an Irishman calling himself Jimmy to show his affinity with the common people) over the future of mankind. *Goodbye Jimmy* has Gray rallying against global warming, the war in Iraq and the tribal factions found among mankind. It is bleakly witty but serves as a reminder that Alasdair Gray's output has become increasingly polemical. He has written two political 'pamphlets' on Scottish politics: *Why Scots Should Rule Scotland* (1992, revised 1997) and (with academic Adam Tomkins) *How We Should Rule Ourselves* (2005). *Why Scots Should Rule Scotland* argues in favour of devolution and compares Scotland with other small nations such as Denmark, Ireland and Finland. It traces the history of Scotland as one of being dominated – both by greed (England) and creed (Calvinism) – and asserts that the Act of Union was essentially an act of colonisation by an England continuing to treat Scotland as a colony out of interest for Scotland's natural resources. He makes a case for Scotland re-imaging itself and does so using a form of Socratic dialogue between a passionate Gray the Pamphleteer and an unidentified Publisher trying to reason with him. It is an engaging read, even if Gray has a tendency to overstate his case. *How We Should Rule Ourselves* continues Gray's cry for an independent republic of Scotland but as a piece of literature it is subdued by Tomkins' academic approach.

Alasdair Gray is a central figure in contemporary Scottish arts and letters. From his debut with *Lanark* in 1981 to his appearance on a Glaswegian-Asian dub record in 2007,[15] he has played a major part in articulating and defining contemporary Scottish identity whilst problematising his country's continual dependence upon England. While his output has been uneven, Gray has served as a stepping stone for other Scottish writers and several of his novels retain their well-deserved place in the Scottish canon. Alasdair

Gray continues to challenge preconceptions of Scottish identity and does so with dark, subversive wit and stark prose. In his own peculiar way, he is as much a Scottish institution as the Kelvingrove art gallery and museum of Gray's beloved West End.

A SMALL INDEPENDENT NATION IS CAPABLE OF A RICH CULTURE[16]

Notes

1. Alasdair Gray, James Kelman and Agnes Owens, *Lean Tales* (London: Jonathan Cape, 1985) p. 283. The postscript is not signed by Gray but is written in his characteristic style.
2. Alasdair Gray, "How This Book Happened", in *The Knuckle End* (Glasgow: Freight Publishers, 2004)
3. Alasdair Gray, *Lanark – A Life in Four Books* (Edingburgh: Canongate, 1981; Canongate Classics edition with postscript by author, 2002)
4. Beat Wischi, *Glasgow Urban Writing and Postmodernism* (Frankfurt: Peter Lang, 1991) p. 68.
5. Angus Calder, *Scotlands of the Mind* (Edinburgh: Luath Press, 2002) (2004) p. xiii.
6. Carl MacDougall, *Writing Scotland: How Scotland's Writers Shaped the Nation* (Edinburgh: Polygon, 2004) p. 100.
7. Alasdair Gray, *1982 Janine* (Edinburgh: Canongate, 1984) (2003) pp. 55-56.
8. See Karina Westermann, *Gray Fingerprints: Alasdair Gray and the Book* (Department of English, University of Copenhagen, 2003) for a discussion of Alasdair Gray and his use of the book as a material/aesthetic object.
9. Alasdair Gray: *Something Leather* (Picador, 1990) pp. 173-74.
10. Kelman's book is the lowest-selling of all Booker Prize winners and was arguably the last experimental novel to win the prize.
11. Raymond Chapman, *The Treatment of Sounds in Language and Literature* (London: Basil Blackwell, 1984) p. 31.
12. See N.F. Blake, "Political, Social and Pedagogical Background to the New Standard" in *A History of the English Language* (London: Macmillan, 1996) for background as to how the Chancery Office dialect became the basis for today's standard written English.
13. Alasdair Gray, *The Book of Prefaces* (London: Bloomsbury, 2000) p. 65-66.
14. Galloway is the author of *The Trick is to Keep Breathing* (1989); an experimental and feminist take on a nervous breakdown. Kennedy has written *Indelible Acts* (2002) and *Paradise* (2004) among other books and is emerging as one of Scotland's most promising writers. Spence is a Glasgow-based poet and novelist.
15. Gray raps/narrates a track called 'Equations of Love' on Asian Underground musician Future Pilot AKA's album released in early 2007.
16. Alasdair Gray, *Why Scots Should Rule Scotland* (Edinburgh: Canongate, 1997) p. 26.

FIVE PASSPORTS AND A BROKEN STONE: TERCENTENARY THOUGHTS IN HONOUR OF EDWARD LHUYD

CHARLES LOCK

ABSTRACT

Waiting at an airport one is likely to have time on one's hands; in them, one might also have a passport. Though seldom studied as texts, passports may, like the best literature, yield to close scrutiny a rich philological interest and a good measure of semantic indeterminacy. This essay, provoked by the anniversary of the union of England and Scotland in 1707, examines a series of passports, issued at ten-year intervals between 1967 and 2007, to find out what it might have meant and what it might yet mean to be the holder of a British passport.

One is known and named by others. Each is alien to the next, as the names of numerous European peoples amply demonstrate: the Welsh, the Vlachs, the Gauls; Galician, Walloon, Gaelic. That nut from Spain, where the best nuts grow, was to the Romans *nux gallica*: fallen on a foreign field, nuts tend to be eaten as imports from elsewhere. Walnuts are 'nuts from Wales', wherever that might mean, or be. What is clear is that we are named not by who we are to ourselves, nor by how we think of ourselves, but by what others call us, and according to what others think of us. Like nuts, we come into nominal being as exports and passengers, crossers of boundaries.

At home, one's identity is given rather than contested. Identity, as a question, a matter of reflection, becomes emphatic only in displacement, is indeed constituted by a movement away from those who take our presence for granted, our identity as subsumed within their own. One answer to Macmorris's celebrated plaint, 'What ish my nation?' (*Henry V*, III iii 63), might come in the form of another question, posed long ago by a lawyer: 'And who is my neighbour?' The neighbour is one who lives in proximity, yet who is not kin, not related, nor of any affinity or necessary likemindedness: neither a friend nor a colleague. We speak of friends and neighbours, as of friends and relations: neighbours are those whom we know in spite of their being neither friends nor relations, whom we are constrained to know by contiguity alone. They are those whose identity ought not to be an issue, even if they have been newcomers, or were once outsiders.

Neighbours can take each other for granted. Nations, though they may be on neighbourly terms, cannot assume similarities of culture or attitude or outlook. Nations must be distinct. What they share are not essential properties (at least, not too many) but needs for material goods. Two nations are two insofar as each perceives the other to be lacking some property (of an immaterial kind) essential to the one. And whatever is lacking in the other, 'essentially' or 'spiritually', can be figured as some positive quality: that's what, in the absence of that special quality, they are constrained to believe over there. By contrast, it is what they have materially that we might both lack and need. Contrary to the received wisdom of political science and economics (and the fears of isolationist politicians), the evidence of recent years suggests that trade does not homogenize nations, does not reduce cultural difference or specificity. As the exchange of material goods, trade makes us aware of other cultures; yet in doing so it enhances the sense, in each nation, of spiritual difference, of what makes one's own unlike any other nation.

Trade creates commodity-envy, and in large measure relies on the cultivation of envy and desire. Yet there is very little concomitant envy of essential otherness, that is to say, of an appreciation of a commodity from elsewhere inducing its consumer to wish to belong 'spiritually' to that alien culture. By commodity-envy I would indicate a trade in which the source of the goods is marked, and held as a positive value: a Volvo, for example, or a Camembert. By contrast we may value a plastic gadget, but we value it for its use, not because it has been made in China. Many of us envy the French their cheeses and their wines, and our envy is collectively expressed and represented in trade. But it is only a rare individual who might wish not to consume French food but to 'become French'. The same can be said for commodity-envy in all its forms: the prevalence of sushi bars does not indicate a widespread wish of westerners to 'become Japanese', or to emulate the Japanese in anything beyond a restricted part of their cuisine. It has long been assumed that there is a direct relationship between the purchasing of commodities from a foreign culture and the valuing of that culture's essential or spiritual life. This seems not to be the case. If one is not a consumer but a convert – having decided that one will become French, or Japanese, or at least engage in serious and extensive mimesis – one would actually have to renounce the envy that motivates trade: if one becomes French, or makes a pretence thereat, one must learn to regard wine and cheese (at least the French ones) in a quotidian manner.

There may be no direct relationship between commodity-envy (in fashion, food, or whatever) and the desire for spiritual emulation of the nation or culture that produces those commodities. The relationship may even be that of an inverse ratio: a nation with which one feels spiritually well-attuned, almost at home, in a neighbourly way (though still distinctly separate), is one that arouses minimal commodity-envy. Within Scandinavia, Danish products count in Sweden or Norway for little beyond their functional worth, and the same can be said *mutatis mutandis* for each nation's exports within Scandinavia. Only outside of the Nordic countries is IKEA a celebrated brand valued for its Swedish and Scandinavian style: in Denmark, however, IKEA is successful not because it is Swedish but because it is functional.

We have for far too long been living under the illusion that international trade and globalization would have an homogenizing effect, benevolently smoothing out the differences between nations and even continents. Global brands do confer on the world's population a common visual language of logo-recognition. This is not to be denied. But the effect of globalization has been the very opposite of assimilation or of that much-hailed 'breaking down of barriers' between people, nations, cultures. Between 1980 and 2000 – the two decades covering the emergence of globalization as a term in general use[1] – the number of member-states of the United Nations did not diminish: rather, it increased, from 154 nations in 1980 to 189 in 2000. In the 1980s and even in the early 90s the idea of a United States of Europe seemed quite plausible, if not inevitable. The term 'Benelux' was in regular use, as if to indicate that these three might as well be treated as one country. Yet we no longer hear of 'Benelux' at all, and European countries today have nothing in common so much as the new-found sense in each of a unique and vulnerable national identity.

The break-up of the Soviet Union is not in itself sufficient to explain the proliferation of new nations. The splitting of Yugoslavia and Czechoslovakia were hardly inevitable, nor, in the case of the latter, anticipated. Thirty years ago one might have predicted that, if ever they regained their independence, the three Baltic republics would unite as a powerful economic force, with Russian as the common language. How distant, even absurd, such a prospect now appears. It is worth remembering such prognoses, to keep an account of misguidance, and to recall how quickly we change our basic assumptions and parameters. The unification of Germany alone supports the counter-argument: with the fragmenting of the Soviet Union, nations were free to unite and to be unified, but only two did so, two whose names in Cold War English – East and West – had declared a divided nation. Officially, however, there was the Federal Republic and the Democratic Republic, each claiming to be the true Germany. In reunification one of them tacitly gave up its claim.

Globalization has been constituted and characterized by a massive increase in the free movement of goods, and a comparable increase in the carefully regulated movement of people. Cheap travel has turned consumers into long-distance tourists. Yet the more we see of the world, and the more nations we visit, the less cosmopolitan we apparently become. This ought not to be a paradox. Not only are there many more nations today than there were twenty-five years ago, when flying was far more expensive, and long-distance travel was largely confined to the middle-classes; there is also a far stronger national sentiment in those countries from which most of the tourists set forth. Indeed, the nations with the greatest number *per capita* of 'global travellers' are among the least tolerant of the others in their own midst, and least flexible in their concepts of *home* and *nation*. *Per capita*, among the best-travelled people in the world are the Danes and the Dutch, whose nations are not the least conspicuous today for the prevalence of nationalist and xenophobic sentiments.

Those who vacation in Bali or Jamaica, and eat exotically when at home, may be less tolerant than people who used to stay put and eat pork pies (or *biksemad*), and are today more likely to be eating pizza or curry, formerly exotic dishes now comprehensively indigenized.[2] This is no paradox once we recognize that commodity-envy may be in inverse ratio to the desire for spiritual emulation of the culture that produces those commodities. (Or destinations: a destination is now a commodity.) The exotic enforces the sense of one's own as different, valuable and vulnerable.

Nations are known by their borders, at their crossings. The border is where the contiguous is also the foreign. In 1707 a national border was dissolved. That was in the early days of capitalism, but in the absence of a contemporary example it is worth thinking about that event in the analytical terms available to us. If Benelux were now one nation, or if Estonia-Latvia-Lithuania formed a state called, let us say, Baltica Magna (or *Zembla*), there would be a contemporary model to examine for signs of analogy with the events of 1707. Yet all we can see around us now are cases to the contrary. It is even conceivable that the border between Scotland and England might be reasserted within the next decade. The growth of separatist sentiment within Scotland has been matched by the development of commodity-envy in England, and massive increases in the movement south (not quite to be reckoned as 'export') of Scotch (than whose, no origin is more forcefully marked, or marketed) and tartan-clad shortbread. There is today greater equality of income, of health and employment figures, of life expectancy, between England and Scotland than ever before. As the two nations become more similar in external or material circumstances they realize their inward separatenesses. (This body-spirit dualism seems to be inescapable in talking of nations and trade and cultures.)

Politicians in favour of the Union (of any union) will always invoke trade as the great sufferer in separatism. They forget that separation is the very condition of trade: there can be no exchange of material goods without spiritually distinct entities between which trade occurs. This, not in the limited sense of trade being by definition across borders, but in the sense that one has to think of a particular commodity as belonging to them, not to us, and as having value because (or although) it is not ours, but theirs; it is in the perception of that difference that both commodity-envy and nationalism thrive.

What happened in 1707 had little to do with trade, or with transport: the great road-building projects reaching into the Highlands were built by Telford after the Union was well established, at the end of the eighteenth century. Without the roads and bridges there could have been little sense of Scotland as a setting for the playing out of Romantic ideology, or as a destination. Scotland was a desirable goal at the very beginnings of tourism as consumption, and in the pursuit of views and landscapes as Romantic commodities. Commodities were not an issue in 1707.[3] The decisive factor was of the essence, of what was spiritually held in common: Scotland and England were united in their Protestantism. Not in spite of all their differences, but only because there were so many things in which they differed, could the Scots and the English agree to be united. This is an old-fashioned, even archaic understanding of the origins of the United Kingdom, but it is one that has been given fresh explanatory force in the work of Linda Colley: the opening chapter of *Britons: Forging the Nation 1707-1837* (1992) is entitled 'Protestants'.

The Scots continued to live much as they had before, to eat the same food (tasteless: oatcakes; or weird: haggis) and wear the same clothes (ridiculous, even indelicate); and so (though much more sensibly, of course) did the English continue in their ways. The pejorative parentheses indicate the stereotypes that worked against any sort of envy or desire to share material goods: the spiritual values of Protestantism were quite enough to be holding in common. It was, one could claim, the absence of trade (as commodity-envy) and a mutual indifference – or even contempt – that preserved the Union. The industrial goods produced in Glasgow in the nineteenth and early twentieth centuries, finding their market in England and abroad, were valued for their function, not because they were 'Scottish'. This is what one might term commodity-contempt, applicable to the Chinese case today, where one takes economic advantage of another nation's products while simultaneously disapproving of a country whose socio-economic arrangements permit the manufacture of such shamefully cheap goods. In this way, also, we see trade as the antithesis of cultural homogenization. Between England and Scotland there was (until very recently) little commodity-envy in either direction. Precisely because there was limited trade in goods conspicuously Scottish (or, conversely, conspicuously English), the Union endured and flourished. (And the English would wonder disapprovingly how the Scots could tolerate the slums of Glasgow.)

* * *

I have in my care (though I do not own: of this, nobody owns her own) a small booklet, hardbound in dark blue boards, with some much-tarnished gold lettering. The very first words at the top of the first page declare:

This passport contains 32 pages

No other book or booklet known to me makes quite such a portentous fuss about its own constitution. Those words are set in roman type. The following words, immediately below, are set in italic:

Ce passeport contient 32 pages

What a curious sort of phrase-book, Alice might remark, that takes itself as the topic of its bearer's tentative stumbling first words in another land, another language.

Below this initial self-declaring confession of size in two tongues we read what is by now obvious, and in capitals: PASSPORT. And below that, in italic uppercase of the same size: *PASSEPORT*. The same size, but that extra *E* makes this word fill more of the line. And below, in small caps, we read

UNITED KINGDOM OF GREAT BRITAIN
AND NORTHERN IRELAND

– the identical form of words, identically lineated, to those we might already have seen on the cover, in tarnished letters, towards the foot. On the cover we also find, at the top, in larger letters, once gilded, 'BRITISH PASSPORT'. Only in English, one might note with some relief, or even complacency, until one spots the large coat of arms occupying the centre, the cover illustration as it were. Here we find words, or at least letters, arranged around the inner crest, apparently from a phrase quite arbitrarily obscured: H O N I S ? ? ? Q U I M ? ? Y P E N S E. And on the swagger at the foot are four whole words, recognizably belonging to the language in which an extra E in required in *passeport*: DIEU ET MON DROIT.

Where are we? And who am I? Back to page 1, where below those eight words repeated from the cover we find, in italics, these:

ROYAUME-UNI DE GRANDE-BRETAGNE
ET D'IRLANDE DU NORD

Below this, in small letters, with long dotted lines awaiting a response, five 'headings':

No. of passport
No. du passeport

Name of bearer
Nom du titulaire

Accompanied by his wife
MAIDEN NAME

Accompagné de sa femme
NÉE

and by   children
et de   enfants

[NB: NÉE, normally italicised in English, is here marked as an English word, lexically repatriated, by being set within French in roman: a typographical detail of exquisite constitutional subtlety, and wit.]

Each of the above pairings is closed by a curly bracket, indicating that only one answer is to be given even though two questions have been asked. And then on one line:

National Status   *Nationalité*

leaving a small space beneath in which we may find, crudely 'printed' as if with a child's set of letters and a purple ink-pad, these defining words:

British Subject:
Citizen of the United
Kingdom and Colonies

Ah! so that's what I was then, in 1967. The previous year England had beaten Germany, with an implicit 'again'. Yes, we beat them: odd how a country when referred to by the third person pronoun becomes *its* – its what? Its people? Residents, inhabitants, citizens, subjects? Nations ought to be 'her', and are such, in formal ceremonial parlance, but nobody ever said that we'd beaten her, whether once or again. And who were 'we'? Were we in 1966 the same 'English team' who had won the War, or were we the British? Never have I heard anyone speak in modern times of the English Army, only of the British Army, yet it was almost always England who had won the War; and if not England, then a unit altogether larger than either Britain or the United Kingdom: 'the Allies'.[4]

In 1967 it was understood that there were two languages required for an act of identification. One tells me and my neighbours and fellow-subjects who I am; the other tells everyone else. As a boy I conflated the language of international diplomacy with the language of the nearest foreign country, the first that one was likely to visit. From the south of England it was hard to get anywhere without passing through France, and this passport is frequently stamped 'Calais'. I had visited France before I'd set foot in any of the other 'nations' of the United Kingdom. And I found myself severely challenged, when first in Wales, because I had entered a country whose road signs were in a language far more 'foreign' than French, yet I had done so without having been asked to produce my passport, had hardly noticed the border as any line of demarcation at all, apart from the dragon welcoming one to Wales: 'Croeso i Cymru' (a dragon with no gate to be at). I was confused partly because I thought I should have been subjected to some control before being allowed among speakers of another language. But I also thought (though I now blush to own it) that people who used such an outlandish combination of letters ought not to be able so easily to enter England. I was hardly the first to feel such sentiments. Daniel Defoe, in his *Tour through the Whole Island of Great Britain* (1724-27), had associated the language with the landscape: 'the names of some of these hills seem'd as barbarous to us, who spoke no Welch, as the hills themselves.'[5]

In 1814 Sir Walter Scott had ascribed similar feelings to Edward Waverley when our English hero finds himself in the Highlands (by courtesy, anachronistically, of Telford's roads and bridges, available for Scott's use, but not there 'sixty years since'):

> It seemed like a dream to Waverley that these deeds of violence should be familiar to men's minds, and currently talked of, as falling within the common order of things, and happening daily in the immediate vicinity, without his

having crossed the seas, and while he was yet in the otherwise well-ordered island of Great Britain.[6]

The story of *Waverley* is set in 1745, the date of the second of the two Jacobite Rebellions, which would mark the last time that any part of Scotland could plausibly be presented as radically different from the rest of Britain. T.M. Devine notes that the defeat of the Highland Clans in 1745 was quickly succeeded by the promotion within the British Army of Highland soldiers as exemplary in courage and endurance, and above all loyalty: 'The speed of the transformation from Jacobite traitors to imperial heroes is astonishing.... Before, the Gael was alien and racially inferior; now, the exploits of the Highland soldier made him a standard-bearer.'[7]

Before 1745 the Highlanders had had no fiercer detractors than the Lowlanders: Scotland was, in the early years of the Union, divided between Highlanders whose life was (or was said to be) organized in a tribal manner, pre-feudal in its primitive loyalties and customs,[8] and Lowlanders, among them those learned persons in Edinburgh and Glasgow who in European reputation rivalled and often excelled their most prominent counterparts in London. After 1745 a reconstruction of the Scottish identity brought together the Highlands and the Lowlands, though there had of course never been a physical border separating these regions, which were and remain divergent states of mind as much as of territory. Scotland was to be presented in terms of compatible and complementary virtues: brain and brawn, the military and the scholarly, the daring and the inventive. Scotland was thus pacified and united, internally, by myth-making: the Highlands most spectacularly by the invention (in the Lowlands) of clans and their tartans, for whose ancient origins there is very little historical or material evidence.[9]

There is hardly a more lucid example of the way in which a partnership, an alliance, a fusion of kingdoms, is to be achieved, less by political or economic means than by symbolic construction. Only when Scotland was joined to England could it be united within itself, learn to be at ease with its own composite identity. The United Kingdom has, to some degree, been held together by such an inclusive image of Scotland, both refined and tough, with strengths both intellectual and industrial. That picture has been constructed not only by the English, but also from within: Edinburgh has had an interest in depicting the Highlands as exotic, as very different from its own highly civilized ways. Walter Scott is symptomatic of this, presenting Waverley's journey to the Lowlands and beyond as itself unremarkable: crossing the border is not an event. The journey from London to Edinburgh and thence to a port on the coast of Angus-shire merits just one sentence.[10]

Scott is following the depiction of the Highlands set out by Smollett:

> The country is amazingly wild, especially towards the mountains, which are heaped upon the backs of one another, making a most stupendous appearance of savage nature, with hardly any signs of cultivation, or even of population. All is sublimity, silence, and solitude [...]. Notwithstanding the solitude that previals among these mountains, there is no want of people in the Highlands [...] if all the Highlanders [...] were united, they could bring into the field an army of forty thousand fighting men [...]. We have lived to see [in 1745] four thousand of them, without discipline, throw the whole kingdom of Great Britain into confusion [...].'[11]

Wales, being smaller, and having been incorporated into 'England and Wales' many centuries earlier, was not a political threat, nor did it have its own cultural centre or its own elite of English-language writers.[12] Those who wrote did so in Welsh, and could be largely ignored by the English. The Welsh had not rebelled against the English since the heroic failure led by Owain Glyndwr in 1400. And yet by the time of the Napoleonic Wars the Welsh were actually more of a problem than the Scots; they were less assimilated, less English-speaking (being in large parts monoglot in Welsh), and much less willing to serve in the British Army: 'North and central Wales especially remained at the start of the nineteenth century the part of Great Britain most resistant to control from the centre.'[13] To a large extent this must be due to the absence within Wales of any centre of learning in the English language. Though Scots as a spoken tongue may be quite distinct from English, the Scots (with a few self-conscious literary exceptions) have always written in English and have in printing followed the grammatical and orthographical rules of London. We might however point out that London must have taken many of its rules from Edinburgh and Glasgow. Scotland has been famous since the eighteenth century for its publishers and printers and editors. The first professorships of English Literature to be established in Britain were not at Oxford or Cambridge but at the Scottish universities.[14] It is to the Scots that we owe much of the development of the printing, publishing and editorial practices throughout the English-speaking world.

The *Encyclopedia Britannica* was first issued in the years around 1770 in Edinburgh, and is one of the earliest enterprises to define itself as British. The British Museum, founded and named in 1753, set a precedent: by 'British' each assert that there is no need to duplicate the effort, whether to have a museum located in Scotland or an encyclopedia edited in England. By contrast, London's National Gallery is matched by a similarly named institution in Edinburgh. The one in Trafalgar Square is responsible for English and Foreign Schools of Painting, Italian, French and so forth. The rest of Britain has no place among the English National Gallery's constituted responsibilities: its first acquisition of a work by a Scottish painter came as recently as 2001.[15]

Wales had no such investment in the English language, and no universities. The Welsh therefore came to depend on those in England: one college at Oxford, Jesus, was founded by a Welshman, Hugh Price, in 1571, and has always attracted students and scholars from Wales. No college at Oxford or Cambridge has ever come to be identified with Scots. Through the endurance of the Welsh language, and the absence in Wales of any centres of learning or publishing in the English language, Wales has retained a strong degree of difference, and of resistance, even though, unlike Scotland, it has never posed a threat to England. Monoglot Welsh speakers would indeed have been disruptive in the British Army, and while there are very few Welsh monoglots today, there is an ever-increasing number of Welsh speakers. It is the separateness and distinctiveness of Welsh identity that leads the Welsh in referenda to make fewer demands than the Scots: the Scots ask for their own parliament with tax-raising powers; the Welsh settle for a 'Welsh Assembly' without fiscal powers, and with fairly vague notions of any powers at all.

Like Edward Waverley, I found that going to Scotland (the Lowlands) was a matter of travelling a bit further than northern England, and that nothing drastic was involved. The glottal and alphabetical trauma induced by a visit to Wales was entirely absent. The Scots may argue, and persuade themselves, that Scots is a language whose history is quite distinct from that of English, having been independently derived from various Norse incursions; the Sassenach, however, will continue to suppose that Scots is a dialect hardly to be distinguished from that of the 'North Country'.

In 2005 the Scottish Parliament took measures to give the Scots a language of their own, and one that could not be treated as merely a dialect of English. The Gaelic Language (Scotland) Act 2005 does not assert that Gaelic is the language of the Scottish people: it is thought to be spoken by no more than 2% of the Scottish population, mostly in the Hebrides. Nor does it confer any rights on Gaelic speakers, who will not be allowed to use Gaelic even in an official context. The Act of 2005 only encourages the use and especially the teaching of Gaelic. In Article 10 (1) of the Act we read that '"The Gaelic language" means the Gaelic language as used in Scotland'. This is the only answer to the obvious question: what is this language? And the answer invites another question: Is 'the Gaelic language' spoken elsewhere? We will defer our attempt to answer this question.

Daniel Defoe must again be invoked. One of the earliest and sharpest of students of the Union of 1707, Defoe wrote of Scotland in the 1720s:

> The Union has seemed to secure her peace, and to encrease her commerce: But I cannot say she has raised her figure in the world at all since that time, I mean as a body; She was before considered as a nation, now she appears no more but as a province, or at best a dominion; she has not lost her name as a place; but as a state, she may be said to have lost it, and that she is now no more than a part of Great Britain in common with other parts of it, of which England it self is also no more. I might enlarge here upon the honour it is to Scotland to be a part of the British Empire, and to be incorporated with so powerful a people under the crown of so great a monarch; their being united in name as one, Britain, and their enjoying all the privileges of, and in common with, a nation who have the greatest privileges, and enjoy the most liberty of any people in the world. But I should be told, and perhaps justly too, that this was talking like an Englishman, rather than like a Briton [...].[16]

The least sensitive (or most anglocentric) reader will note that while Scotland has ceased to be a nation, as has England, yet Scotland should be glad to be joined to what Defoe persists in calling 'a nation', one whose people enjoy the most liberty. England's standing as a nation has not been diminished: unlike Scotland, England is not reduced to the status of province or dominion. Everything here depends on the power and the location of discourse: for thinkers of the Scottish Enlightenment there was little virtue in distinctness as such: one might now speak of the Scottish Enlightenment, but the idea of a separate Enlightenment is a contradiction in terms: our special way of reasoning: a local illumination? It is a fact too little stressed that Scotland was the centre of Enlightenment in the English language. England and Scotland had in common not only Protestantism but also English.

Setting the claims of the Stuarts against those of the Hanoverians, David Hume wrote in 1748 'Of the Protestant Succession', with memories of the '45 Rebellion still fresh. Hume could well articulate the attractiveness of the Stuarts, not least to the Scots. Yet the restoration of the Stuarts would have rendered the Protestant kingdom vulnerable to the possibility of a Catholic monarch, and so, although his heart is clearly not in it, Hume prefers the Hanoverian settlement. In *Waverley*, Scott clearly endorses Hume's position, while amplifying its regrets and qualifications.[17] Again dualism is at work: the Highlands form a fictional territory of Scott's creation that would inspire the invention of 'Romantic hinterlands', exotic yet 'within reach', within the national borders, all over Europe: the Alps, Bavaria, the Black Forest, Brittany, Provence, Andalusia, Sicily, the Caucasus. Many of these peripheral territories are associated with the Celtic fringe: peripheral territories of otherness created in the imagination, only after transport and centralized governance have done their civilizing and homogenizing work.

The Highlands, like other richly imagined peripheries, became exotic when they ceased to be foreign. What Scott made of the Highlands, Pushkin and Lermontov (formerly Lermont, of Scottish descent) did for the Caucasus, but only after the region had been incorporated into the Russian Empire. 'Foreign' is itself a problematic term. On p. 4 of the 1967 passport one reads (and this is by far the most substantial statement in the booklet not to be 'repeated' in French) that this is 'Valid for all parts of the Commonwealth and for all Foreign Countries'. No attempt is made to translate this into French. One notes that by this definition there are no Commonwealth countries: the Commonwealth is one unity divided into parts, territories, provinces or dominions. These were often gathered together under the term 'overseas': a word that for dwellers on an island would cover almost everything. But 'overseas' has a specific imperial sense (dating back to c. 1900), to mean those places around the world that were not part of the British Isles but were not foreign either. The names of the two airlines captured this neatly: British European Airways (BEA) and the British Overseas Aircraft Corporation: BOAC originally serviced only imperial routes. And those parts, however far away they may be, are not to be regarded as foreign. The word Commonwealth in the passport is already unmodified by 'British': it is merely by implication that 'British' is to be understood.

Within the British Government the so-called Foreign Secretary is an abbreviated form for the person properly styled 'The Secretary of State for Foreign and Commonwealth Affairs': she is responsible for the Foreign and Commonwealth Office, and it is clear that whatever belongs to the Commonwealth cannot, by this definition, be foreign. By the same token, Commonwealth members have no embassies in London: London is not a foreign capital to which an ambassador can be sent on a mission. In London one finds instead the High Commission of each member of the Commonwealth, a home-base, as it were, connecting the centre to the periphery of a single vast but unitary domain. Such a notion of the Commonwealth as the continuation of empire by subtly different means (and at considerably reduced cost to the 'mother country') was already fragile (if not absurd) by 1967. Yet these arrangements point to a 'spiritual essence' (the English language, Protestantism, the love of liberty, democracy, the rule of law, a sense of fair play, and so on) that is utterly indifferent to proximity or contiguity. Another of the paradoxes of globalization is that, despite the astonishing advances in transport and communications over recent years, our political unions, blocs and affiliations have become strictly contiguous. With the European Union, the North American Free Trade Area, the Association of South-East Asian Nations, the Organization of African Unity, we have seen the end of empires on which the sun would never set.

The globally non-contiguous vision implied in the statement – 'Valid for all parts of the Commonwealth and for all Foreign Countries' – is no longer found in the passport issued in 1977, though it is replaced by another statement (also only in English), to the effect that 'Holder has the right of abode in the United Kingdom' without modification or limitation. Which united kingdom might that be? Much depends on implication. Those odd names, the United Kingdom and the United States (and, formerly, the Soviet Union), are alone among national names in dropping, for the short form, the name of the territory on which the nation is situated. These ought to remind us of an accuracy of nominal purpose too often ignored. Denmark is, properly speaking, not Denmark, nor is France France. Properly speaking one should refer to the Republic of France and the Kingdom of Denmark. Postage stamps ('RF') and the currency are not slaves to anachronism: they are stubborn witnesses to a necessary precision whose purpose is generally forgotten. In abbreviating the full name of the nation to the name of the territory it occupies, one is assuming a constitutional relation between territory and state that is quite unjustified. It is in fact to do what Defoe observes had been done to Scotland: 'she has not lost her name as a place; but as a state, she may be said to have lost it.' What makes the state is not the territory, nor the name of its inhabitants, but the state's constitution as a kingdom or republic, a dominion or a federation: a constitution that may be ratified internally but that can be recognized only by other states.

The 1987 passport is marked by Mrs. Thatcher's decidedly unfriendly British Nationality Act of 1981. There is no statement in this passport to the effect that the bearer has the right of abode anywhere. I find my 'National Status' no longer described or defined as 'British Subject: Citizen of the United Kingdom and Colonies' but as 'British Citizen'. Note 2, inside back cover, informs me that 'British citizens have the right of abode in the United Kingdom' whereas 'British subjects' do not. I was puzzled: I thought that I would still be a British subject, as well as being a British citizen. Yet here the term 'British subject' would seem to be hard to distinguish from 'illegal immigrant'.

The passport of 1997 looks completely different, bound in soft rather than hard covers, in the maroon colour of what was then named the 'European

Community'. Here I no longer have a national status at all. I am not required to belong to a nation but I must have a 'Nationality'. Mine is 'British Citizen'. This is truly perplexing: what then ish my nation? 'British City'? The lexical change from subject to citizen has marked the greatest constitutional shift in the formation and disintegration of my identity: as a schoolboy I recall being told, insistently, that only those who belong to a republic can be termed citizens: those in a monarchy must be subjects. The French are properly to be called citizens, we were told, with some disdain.

On 3 May 2007 Her Majesty, Queen Elizabeth the Second, visited Virginia to commemorate the four hundredth anniversary of the founding of the Jamestown settlement. In an address to a Joint Session of the Virginia General Assembly these pioneering colonists were described in Her Majesty's very own words as 'a small group of British citizens'. This is a royal anachronism of disturbing extent, for each of the words 'British' and 'citizens' is, on its own, problematic when applied to 1607. The combination 'British citizen' is unheard of until the 1970s: the phrase entered official usage only in 1981. When Her Majesty had previously visited Jamestown, in 1957, for the 350th anniversary, Her Majesty would have spoken of those settlers as 'English men and women'. Was there a Scot among them, or a Welsh man or woman? (They were from East Anglia, mostly from Suffolk.)

Who, anyway is this person, Her Majesty, who speaks on behalf of us, Her – Her what? Her citizens? This is the Sovereign's full title:

> Elizabeth yr Ail, trwy ras Duw, o Deymas Unedig Prydain Fawr a Gogledd Iwerddon a'i Theymasoedd a'i Thiriogaethan eraill, Brenhines, Pennaeth y Gymanwlad, Amddiffynydd y Ffydd

or, as the monarch is styled in another language than Welsh:

> Elizabeth the Second, by the Grace of God, of the United Kingdom of Great Britain and Northern Ireland and of Her other Realms and Territories Queen, Head of the Commonwealth, Defender of the Faith.

One notes that, in the official style, the only territory that is named is 'Northern Ireland': the Kingdom of England, the Kingdom of Scotland and the Principality of Wales are comprised under 'the United Kingdom of Great Britain', which might otherwise be synonymous with the British Isles were it not for that part of Ireland that is not Northern, yet calls itself the Republic of Ireland, not of Southern Ireland only. Yet Northern Ireland is merely a territorial description: it is not its own kingdom or principality nor is it known as anything but a 'province'. It is not even Ulster, lacking as it does three of the counties that made up the north-eastern quarter of ancient Ireland. Title to Northern Ireland has always been hard to establish and define, and it causes trouble in the very title of Her Majesty: 'Ireland' names the incoherence or inadequacy of all political definitions of 'British', of all attempts to use 'British' to pose the normative unity of the British Isles (a territory) with Great Britain (a state).

So far the languages used in a British passport have been just two: French and English. This simplicity has not endured. Almost the first words to be read in the British passport issued in 1997 are these:

> Det europaeiske Faellesskab

Danish has pride of place among the languages of the nine other members of that group known in English, and in large type, as THE EUROPEAN COMMUNITY. The list of the nine names of the 'member-states' of the European Community in their eight languages is arranged neither by the name of the nation nor by that of the language. Most of the languages in which the European Community is known to its members are easily identified, and the name recognized, but two are likely to cause trouble. One is in Greek letters (we suppose that must be the Greek for it), and the other says: 'An Comhphobal Eorpach'.

Below this we find in, large type, 'United Kingdom of Great Britain and Northern Ireland' and on the right, in small type, that nation (or 'member-state'?) as it is known in the eight languages of the other European Community members, beginning 'Det forenede Kongerige Storbritannien og Nordirland'. One of them reads: 'Ríocht Aontaithe na Breataine Móire agus Thuaisceart Éireann'. No longer is everything stated in two languages, 'one's own' and French; instead, everything is in as many languages as the Community's members are officially supposed to speak: 'Dette pas består af 32 (nummererede) sider'. Where has Alice found herself now? And, as the Community becomes a union, and acquires twenty-seven members, where in this profusion of self-defining, self-affirming, self-glorifying polyglottism will there be room for details about Alice, or me? How might this tell me or others who I am, or explain away my confusion as to whether I am a citizen or a subject: might I be a citizen of both Europe and the United Kingdom, and yet be also a British subject, or a subject of Her Britannic Majesty? And in how many languages might this need to be explained?

The passport issued in 2007 has quite given up the attempt to present itself as a passport for all Europeans, conveying information in all the official tongues of the EU. The basic notes are given in 22 languages, as is the self-adverting statement that 'This passport contains 32 pages' though the pages are no longer said to be numbered and are in fact unnumbered. (What sort of security might be enhanced by the eradication of pagination? Have they no sense of the basic bibliographical value of collation?) Instead this new passport (which does in fact consist of 32 pages) has taken advantage of the minority languages of the United Kingdom to disguise and promote a thoroughly insular withdrawal from Europe.[18] For the first time French is no longer prominent, and is used only as the motto of the Order of the Garter. This is no longer a *passeport*, and what it is is given in three languages, none of them French:

> Pasbort
>
> Cead-siubhail
>
> PASSPORT

First Welsh, last English. And in the middle, what? Is help to be found in the order? It is not in alphabetical order of the name for 'passport', nor of the languages, even as they name themselves: Cymraig ... English. Between them would come Eireann: is this Irish? But the Irish call their language Gaelic or Gaeilge, so that theory will not hold. Need we ask why only one of these is in uppercase lettering: uppercase but last? We must be concerned at the fact that none of these languages is printed in italics. This would imply, by all the rules of textual editing, that all the words are from the same language. A somewhat desperate confusion is evident: foreignness in philology has been equated with foreignness of nation. As these are not the tongues of foreign nations, the assumption seems to be, they cannot be foreign tongues. Not even to each other? Not to English?

Discrimination is not made by the facial opposition *italic*-roman, but by letter-case. At the top of the page in uppercase we read

> EUROPEAN UNION

and then, where we'd expect the same in French, we (to say nothing of the French) are startled to find:

> Yr Undeb Ewropeaidd

Aonadh Eòrpach

We may remember Eòrpach, though in 1997 it lacked the grave accent, and modified something else: 'An Comhphobal Eorpach'. Then it was the European Community, now it is the European Union. So is this Irish? But in making this connection we must reckon that the point-of-view, the personality, the subject-position of this Irish writing has been radically altered. This would not be the representative language of the Republic of Ireland, one of the member-states of the European Union: this would be the language of the province of Northern Ireland, one of the minority languages of the United Kingdom. Yet it is a language ignored, even disdained, by the Protestant Loyalists whose majority status ensures that Northern Ireland remain part of the United Kingdom, and whose Protestantism remains even today at the very heart of that loyalty. Those who would identify with this language are likely to be a small minority of Irish Nationalists, who would be Roman Catholics and in favour of a united Ireland achieved by removing Northern Ireland from the United Kingdom. If Ireland were to be unified as a Republic, the rule of contiguity would score another triumph. However, the name of the United Kingdom would not be compromised but would be rendered, along with Her Majesty's title, a great deal more coherent.

Which brings us to the centre of the first page (unpaginated):

UNITED KINGDOM
OF GREAT BRITAIN AND
NORTHERN IRELAND

Teyrnas Gyfunol Prydain Fawr
a Gogledd Iwerddon

Rioghachd Aonaichte Bhreatainn
is Eireann a Tuath

The United Kingdom is named in Gaelic, as from within its borders, in rather different words from those ascribed to the Republic of Ireland as a member-state of the European Union. For the Gaelic of the Republic of Ireland the United Kingdom had been (in 1997) 'Riocht Aontaithe na Breataine Móire agus Thuaisceart Éireann'. It would seem that the Republic of Ireland acknowledges 'Breataine Móire' while these other Gaelic speakers will not concede the 'Móire': Britain, not Great Britain. It is generally forgotten that Britain was first named 'great' not by virtue of its empire or its history, but to describe in 1603 the union in James the First's person of England, Wales,

Scotland and Ireland: the name is purely territorial, and in its earlier French form distinguished the large group of islands from the smaller peninsular also named *Bretagne*, known in English as Brittany. (Only the French risk ambiguity whenever they omit the '*Grande*': much of what's less than *cordiale* in European history may be illuminated by this detail.)

The Irish supposition has turned out to be a red (or green) herring, or a shaggy dog story. Research has led me to the information that the language on the passport is Gaelic, as I'd supposed, but not the Gaelic with which we had become familiar on our passports in the 1990s. The Gaelic of 2007 is a consequence of the Act passed by the Scottish Parliament in 2005: '"The Gaelic language" means the Gaelic language as used in Scotland'. It would seem, to a cynical Sassenach, that for the Scots their Gaelic is, alas, just as much a dialect as is their Scots. After no little work, we have learnt that the British passport now defines and announces the full name of the United Kingdom in English, Welsh and the Gaelic language as used in Scotland.

The Welsh language has enjoyed an impressive and welcome revival over the past half-century and more. It has the status of an official language in Wales; its speakers have the right to use Welsh in court, and all children in Wales are encouraged to learn Welsh at school. Significantly these rights were conferred by the parliament of the United Kingdom sitting in Westminster, through the Welsh Language Act of 1967, not by a devolved assembly in Wales. By what authority, I wonder, is Scots Gaelic used on my passport? Was the matter ever discussed at Westminster, or was its use merely conceded at some level of officialdom? I had supposed that the inclusion of all the languages of the EU on the 1997 passport had been debated and approved in Brussels or Strasbourg, or both. Was approval sought from the EU when the British passport became more linguistically insular than it has ever been before? Not the least of the absurdities of the new passport is that its non-English languages will be unknown and unspoken all around the world: it's quite something these days to attain global unrecognizability. These languages could be read only where the British can go without taking a passport, without crossing a frontier.

While I'm pleased that the Celtic languages are being recognized and used within the United Kingdom, I anticipate the occasion when a customs official asks a British traveller to explain what these funny words mean and how we can be sure that they do not encrypt all sorts of nefarious messages. Could any British passport holder respond, honestly and in the affirmative, to the question: And did you pack your passport yourself? It contains all sorts of unfamiliar matter, and I'd be quite unable to explain how it got there.

*   *   *

It was on an early visit to London that, as a schoolboy in the 1960s, I felt the tension in the Union, a sense of conflict between England and Scotland stronger than any I've experienced in visiting Scotland itself. Under the Coronation Chair in Westminster Abbey was the Stone of Scone, first placed there soon after Edward I had seized it from the Scots in 1296: it was the stone on which all Scottish monarchs had been crowned. Its presence in the Abbey would have been scandalous until 1603, though it was no longer an anomaly once the two kingdoms had been united in the person of James, the First of England, the Sixth of Scotland.

In 1950, on Christmas Day, the Stone was stolen from Westminster Abbey in an act that could be viewed either as profoundly sacrilegious or as a high-spirited prank. The culprits – quickly identified, though never charged – were four young persons, some of whom were to become leading figures in the Scottish National Party. In the course of its removal to Scotland the stone was broken, though it seems to have been reassembled after its recovery and before being displayed once more in Westminster Abbey. There was no visible sign of a crack.

The Coronation Chair, originally designed to enclose and frame the Stone of Scone, unites two kingdoms, holds them in an almost palpable tension. Yet in 1996, by way of marking the seven hundredth anniversary of its seizing, the British Government decided that the Stone should be 'returned' to Scotland. It would be brought back to the Abbey only for a coronation ceremony. The Coronation Chair is now quite emptied of its significance: its peculiar shape holds only a vacancy. And the Stone now rests neglected, even forlorn, in Edinburgh Castle, no longer a force radiating tension, focussing indignation.

A stone at home is just a stone, hardly to be reckoned a stone at all. Like a nut, a name, a person, a subject. For identity depends not only on displacement, but also on what inevitably follows displacement: a sense of injustice or of inadequate recognition. Since Woodrow Wilson proclaimed self-determination as 'an imperative principle' of international politics, it has been generally acknowledged as 'a Good Thing', and as a goal for all frustrated minorities seeking to build their own just society. What we may soon be learning, in international affairs as well as on the personal level, is that it is an excess of self-determination that leads to a crisis of identity. Whether as an English subject or as a British citizen I miss the Stone of Scone from its place in the Abbey: most of all I miss the crack that cannot be seen, the sundering that (dis)embodies the fracture that runs through every united entity. No border, no limit, no boundary should forget that it was always a fracture, though it may once have been invisible. The least explicable aspect of national boundaries is that they are in general admirably constant and stable; yet they endure not because they contain and limit and confine, but because they give passage, as my passport still requests, in the name of Her Majesty, 'freely without let or hindrance'. Inside the border there is no need for identification: only in passage do I learn who I am, do I become aware of that hidden fissure, that inner misfitting, without which there's no knowing.

Between January and May of 2007, the period covering the three hundredth anniversary of the key dates of its creation and constitution, the United Kingdom did little officially, and less spontaneously, by way of commemoration. In May 2007, the Scottish electorate for the first time gave its vote to the Scottish National Party whose very purpose is to divide the two kingdoms, and presumably to turn the northern one into a republic. (I trust the Stone of Scone will then be returned to the Abbey as surplus to requirements, to be displayed in London, now capital merely of England, as yet another relic.)

There is another anniversary of 1707 that we ought to be celebrating. It was in that year that Edward Lhuyd (né Lloyd, c. 1660-1709), Keeper of the Ashmolean Museum in Oxford and formerly a student at Jesus College, published the first volume of his extraordinarily extensive researches into British and Celtic antiquities: *Archaeologica Britannica*. This volume, the *Glossography*, based on his travels around Wales, Cornwall, Scotland, Ireland and Brittany, presents the argument that all the 'Gallic' (or Gaulish) languages were to be regarded as members of the Celtic family, and that the Celtic languages could be divided into two main groups: the Brythonic (Welsh, Cornish, Breton) and the Goidelic (Irish Gaelic, Scots Gaelic, Manx). Edward Lhuyd is the founder of our sense of the Celtic, not only as a group of languages but as a mode of being, not quite a form of civilization, but a way of living on the periphery, in a space just beyond the reach of reason and empire, and of globalization. The United Kingdom was shaped by the forces of Enlightenment and Protestantism: in being well-regulated its world was intended to be disenchanted. Enchantment, such as befell Edward Waverley, could be treacherous. In Hume or in Scott we can register the stark polarity of the choice between Stuarts and Hanoverians: at the thought of the Hanoverians has any heart ever missed a beat?

The Celtic endows the world with a lingering trace of enchantment. Without the Celtic there would hardly have been, as an alternative to the Enlightenment, that celebration and valorization of mystery that we call Romanticism. As grounds for separatism or for a national identity the Celtic, whether as language or as more than a language, seems inadequate; yet the Celtic has provided a refuge, an obscure unlocatable elsewhere for the imagination of Europe. It is a place to which no passport gives passage. The Celtic provides few commodities and is subject to little commodity-envy. Yet, according to the inverse ratio that we have outlined, the Celtic evokes an exceptional sense of spiritual affinity in those who might otherwise be terminally disenchanted. Let us therefore honour the memory of Edward Lhuyd and his *Glossography*, published in 1707 and still giving shape to our lives. The Celtic simultaneously inspires division and solaces the imagination: those who warm to its divergent summonings are liable to be called (by the voice of efficiency and reason, progress and globalization) nuts.

Notes

[1] The widespread use of the term can be dated to the article by Theodore Levitt, 'Globalization of markets', published in the *Harvard Business Review* in 1983.

[2] On the subject of curry, for many years now the most commonly catered dish in the United Kingdom, it may be noted that 'Vindaloo!' as the chant of English football supporters seems to entail few warm or positive feelings towards people of South Asian background.

[3] That is to say, the exchange of commodities between England and Scotland was not significant; the economic attraction for the Scots was the access that Union would provide, not to England but to England's markets, in North America and elsewhere.

[4] One cannot calculate the damage inflicted on the Union by the absence of a team representing the United Kingdom in football, rugby or cricket. Were it not for 'the England team' the flag of St. George would be flown only from a few churches on the 23rd of April. The power of sport in the past half-century, and its virtual monopoly over the popular expression of national sentiment, has doomed the Union Jack to redundancy outside of royal occasions.

[5] Daniel Defoe, *A Tour Through England and Wales* (Dent: Everyman, 1928), Vol. 2, p. 60.

[6] Walter Scott, *Waverley; or, 'Tis Sixty Years Since*, ed. C. Lamont (Oxford World's Classics, 1986) pp. 72-3 (the closing paragraph of Chapter XV).

[7] T.M. Devine, *The Scottish Nation 1700-2007* (Penguin, 2006) p. 240.

[8] Smollett laments that despite all attempts to weaken the clan system, 'the original attachment still remains and is founded on something prior to the feudal system': Tobias Smollet, *The Expedition of Humphry Clinker* (1772), ed. Lewis M. Knapp, Oxford UP. 1966, p. 354

[9] See Hugh Trevor-Roper, 'The Highland Tradition in Scotland' in Eric Hobsbawm & Terence Ranger, *The Invention of Tradition* (Cambridge University Press, 1983).

[10] See *Waverley*, p. 30 (the opening paragraph of Chapter VII).

[11] Smollett, pp. 253-254. Smollett explains the Highlanders' prowess in physiological terms: 'They do not walk like the generality of mankind, but trot and bounce like deer, as if they moved upon springs.'

12. Wales was under English rule from the early Middle Ages, but it was only in 1746 that the 'Berwick and Wales Act' stipulated that in all official documents 'England' should be understood to include Wales. This portion of the 1746 Act was revoked by the Welsh Language Act of 1967.
13. Linda Colley, *Britons: Forging the Nation 1707-1837* (1992; 2nd ed., Yale, 2004), p. 295.
14. See Robert Crawford, *Devolving English Literature* (Oxford, 1992).
15. The painting is Henry Raeburn's portrait of the Ferguson brothers known as 'the Archers': see the (English) National Gallery's Press Release, May 2001. At almost the same time (2000) the Tate Gallery reconfigured itself in two parts, Tate Modern and Tate Britain, the latter recalling the Tate's formal name (and purpose) at its founding in 1897: The National Gallery of British Art.
16. See Ian Duncan, 'Hume, Scott and the "Rise of Fiction"', *Angles on the English-Speaking World*, Vol. 3, 2003, pp. 63-76
17. Defoe, *Tour*, Vol. 2, p. 137.
18. The withdrawal is just that, into the background: the names for the European Union and the United Kingdom in all the official languages of the EU are present, very faintly, as the forgery-proof ground of the page.

NOTES ON CONTRIBUTORS

Graham Caie is Professor of English Language and Associate Dean at Glasgow University. He is vice-chairman of the Board of Trustees of the National Library of Scotland and of the Scottish Texts Society and an advisor to the Scottish Arts Council. Recent books are on medieval texts in manuscript context and critical editions of Chaucer's *Man of Law's Tale* and the Old English poem *Judgement Day II*.

Henrik Halkier is Professor of Regional and Tourism Studies at Aalborg University. His research interests include regional policy in Britain and Europe, place branding, and knowledge processes in tourism development. His recent publications include *Institutions, Discourse and Regional Development. The Scottish Development Agency and the Politics of Regional Policy* (Brussels: PIE Peter Lang, 2006).

Charles Lock, Professor of English Literature at the University of Copenhagen, is a European citizen not singularly attached to any one of its nations: he is most at home among documents no longer valid.

David McCrone is Professor of Sociology, and co-director of the University of Edinburgh's Institute of Governance. He is a Fellow of the Royal Society of Edinburgh, and a Fellow of the British Academy. He coordinated the research programme funded by The Leverhulme Trust on Constitutional Change and National Identity (1999-2004), and on National Identity, Citizenship and Social Inclusion (2006-2010). His books include *Has Devolution Delivered?* (2006); *Living in Scotland: social and economic change since 1980* (2004); *Understanding Scotland: the sociology of a nation* (2001) and *The Sociology of Nationalism: tomorrow's ancestors* (1998).

Dr Steve Murdoch is Reader in History at the University of St Andrews. His two monographs are *Britain, Denmark-Norway and the House of Stuart 1603-1660* (East Linton, Tuckwell Press, 2000) and *Network North: Scottish Kin, Commercial and Covert Associations in Northern Europe, 1603-1746* (Leiden, Brill, 2006). He has edited four volumes on aspects of Scottish relations with the wider world and is currently working on a monograph entitled *Scottish Privateering, 1513-1713* (Leiden, Brill forthcoming 2008).

Jens Rahbek Rasmussen studied history at the University of Copenhagen where he is now Senior Lecturer in British history. He also has a Master's degree in interpreting from the Copenhagen Business School and spent five years working for the European Community in Brussels. He has published widely on Scandinavian and British history and has recently edited a collection of essays placing the British bombardment of Copenhagen in 1807 in both the Danish and the international context. At present he is writing a survey of British history aimed at foreign students.

Jørgen Sevaldsen is a lecturer in the Department of English, Germanic and Romance Studies at the University of Copenhagen. His research interests lie in the fields of contemporary British history and modern Anglo-Danish relations. Among his recent publications are *Britain and Denmark, Political, Economic and Cultural Relations in the 19th and 20th Centuries* (ed., 2003); *Churchill: Statsmand og Myte* (2004), and *Montgomery: Danmarks Befrier* (2007).

Robert Christian Thomsen is associate professor and director of the Canadian Studies Centre, Institute of Language, Literature and Culture, University of Aarhus. His research interests include national and regional identity-building processes in Britain and Canada, and destination images in tourism. He is currently finishing a monograph on autonomism in Scotland and Newfoundland, to be published by McGill-Queen's University Press.

Paul Ward is Professor of British History at the University of Huddersfield. He is interested in national identities in the United Kingdom in the twentieth century. His publications include *Red Flag and Union Jack* (1998), *Britishness since 1870* (2004) and *Unionism in the United Kingdom 1918-1974* (2005). He is currently writing a book on Welshness and Britishness.

Karina Westermann is a graduate of the University of Copenhagen. She is interested in print culture (particularly textual materiality) and contemporary British fiction with occasional detours into poetry. Karina Westermann lives and works in Glasgow.

John R. Young is a Senior Lecturer in History at the University of Strathclyde in Glasgow. He has published on early modern Scottish History and is the author of *The Scottish Parliament 1639-1661: A Political and Constitutional Analysis (Edinburgh, 1996)*.

FORTHCOMING ISSUES

- *Cultures of Childhood*
  Volume 8, 2008
  Editor: Charles Lock

- *English in Denmark: Language Policy, Internationalization and University Teaching*
  Volume 9, 2009
  Editors: Peter Harder et al.

- *Crossing Boundaries: Religion and the Arts*
  Volume 10, 2010
  Editor: Inge Birgitte Siegumfeldt